The "You" Effect

Tom Trush
P.O. Box 90993
Phoenix, AZ 85066
Phone: 602.305.6755
E-mail: tom@writewaysolutions.com
Website: http://www.writewaysolutions.com

Editor: Linda Sandow

Cover design by Amanda Moore

First Printing: April 2012

ISBN-10: 1470039133
EAN-13: 9781470039134

The "You" Effect

How to Transform Ego-Based Marketing Into Captivating Messages That Create Customers

by
Tom Trush

Praise for Tom Trush
and The "You" Effect ...

"A Must-Read for Every Professional and Business Owner Marketing to Today's Skeptical, Distrusting Buyers"

*"Tom Trush's **The 'You' Effect** is the finest collection of practical marketing tips I've ever seen. No dry-as-dust theory here. Rather, Tom fuses time-proven marketing principles with today's technological innovations. As a result, you discover how to create and implement a highly persuasive message that attracts inquiries, orders and profits. These tested strategies — combined with Tom's common-sense approach — make this book a must-read for every professional and business owner marketing to today's skeptical, distrusting buyers."*

Trey Ryder
Education-Based Marketing Specialist
http://www.treyryder.com

"Don't Be Surprised If Some People Criticize (and Then Copy) Your Marketing Efforts"

"Tom's tips are easy to understand and implement because they enhance activities you're already doing. He puts unique twists on common-sense approaches. This book is a great read for entrepreneurs eager to market their businesses with educational strategies. But a word of warning: Tom's strategies aren't the traditional tactics your competitors are used to seeing. So don't be surprised if some people criticize (and then copy) your marketing efforts. A very powerful marketing book sits in your hands — use it to your advantage."

Ben Koeller, CPA
Certified Public Accountant
http://www.btkcpa.com

"Hardcore Money-Getting Strategies That Have Stood the Test of Time"

*"Tom Trush's **The 'You' Effect** covers many of the (often) not-talked-about, totally undisputed, and universal principles for raw, hardcore money-getting strategies that have stood the test of time. This book is a must-read for any entrepreneur."*

Charles E. Gaudet II
Creator of the Predictable Profits™ Methodology
http://www.predictableprofits.com

"Sound Business Rules That Should Be at the Foundation of Every Marketing Piece"

"The book showcases simple, easy-to-implement ideas to make your marketing work harder. Tom's ability to think about a customer's perspective ensures copy is always relevant to the reader and drives action. These are sound business rules that should be at the foundation of every marketing piece."

Steve Harney
Owner
Full Circle Marketing & Interactive
http://www.thinkfullcircle.com

"Will Fundamentally Shift Your Thinking and Could Well Transform Your Business"

*"As an Internet marketing consultant, I've worked with clients all over the world for nearly 20 years. The message Tom delivers in **The 'You' Effect** is the essence of what most start-ups — and long-established businesses — miss in their branding. Read this book. It will fundamentally shift your thinking and could well transform your business."*

Andy Renk
President
Venturian Marketing
http://www.venturian.net

To the world's teachers (especially my wife, Michelle; mom, Linda; and dad, Bill) — the classroom marketers who work every day to persuade the most merciless audiences you could ever imagine.

Contents

How to Transform Ego-Based Marketing Into Captivating Messages That Create Customers

Part II: Building a Bond and Creating Trust

Part III: Crafting Your Marketing Message

Part IV: Using Specific Marketing Mediums

Introduction

The marketing game has changed ...

But many high-level executives behind big brands and major corporations still haven't noticed. They're blinded by a desire to showcase the greatness behind their companies.

That's okay, though, because this ego-based marketing approach means more opportunity for you.

The reality is the Internet has become the center of the marketing universe. These days, people wanting to buy a product or service first turn to their laptops, smartphones, iPads and a slew of other Internet-enabled devices.

And they don't have to look far. After all, these technological tools often sit within an arm's reach.

So why are prospective buyers so eager to search online? What are they looking for?

Well, since you're also a consumer participating in today's marketing game, the answer is probably pretty clear ...

People go to the Internet for useful content that helps them make informed decisions.

Right?

The Internet has transformed the buying process, producing prospects who are more educated about your product or service than ever before. This creates problems for companies that rely on pushing one-sided marketing messages to the masses.

When you consider all the distractions competing for your prospects' attention each day, it's no wonder self-centered promotional materials are so easy to ignore. After all, why would prospects care about your company's objectives when they have their own needs and desires to worry about?

Today, your role as a marketer is similar to a publisher. You must produce and deliver valuable content when and where prospects need it. Of course, creating content requires a complete understanding of your target audience. What works is focusing on your prospects' problems. What fails is force-feeding facts about what you sell.

As you read the following pages, you'll discover how to create *The "You" Effect*™ — a process that transforms ego-based marketing into captivating messages that create customers. Along the way, you'll see how changing your perspective on prospects can position you as an industry authority, deliver higher returns on your marketing investments and allow you to reach larger audiences with less effort.

The foundation for *The "You" Effect*™ is based on a simple and extremely persuasive word you'll learn more about in Chapter 1.

Similar to my first book, **The Reluctant Writer's Guide to Creating Powerful Marketing Materials: 61 Easy Ideas to Attract Prospects and Get More Customers**, the tips, tricks and techniques are presented in small, bite-sized chunks. Each chapter is an idea originally shared with subscribers of my e-mail newsletter and blog.

You can read the following pages cover to cover or just pick and choose ideas that grab your attention. Either way, you'll gain copywriting and marketing insight you can begin using today to generate more responses from your marketing.

But before we begin, here's one final thought to remember:

You'll never go wrong in your marketing when you show compassion and a desire for helping people.

Now let's get going!

Tom Trush
Direct-Response Copywriter and Marketing Strategist

Wait, one more thing ...

Within seconds of starting the next chapter, you'll begin evaluating your current marketing efforts — the reaction is only natural. So here's a quick three-question marketing quiz to help with your assessment and ensure you're positioned for marketing success:

Question #1: The easiest way to turn your prospects into customers is to ...

    A. Put your "brand" (i.e., company name, logo, etc.) in front of them as much as possible
    B. Offer the lowest price or a discount
    C. Make sure they're eager to solve their problem(s)
    D. Create convincing copy that results in more action on your offers

Answer: C

You'll have an easier time persuading prospects who don't need to be educated about the need for your product or service.

As for your company name or logo, since neither one offer benefits to your prospects, they have no effect on purchasing decisions. Also, low pricing and discounting requires higher sales volume, often resulting in more effort and money spent on marketing.

And, finally, regardless of how convincing your copy is, prospects will never take action on anything they don't want to do. You can only capitalize on an unfilled need or desire.

Question #2: The primary reason for having strong marketing copy is to …

    A. Establish credibility and trust with your prospects
    B. Get more leads
    C. Produce additional sales and increase revenue
    D. Make Tom happy

Answer: A

You're at a disadvantage the instant you put your marketing message in front of your prospects. Many know you're trying to sell them something, so they immediately don't like or trust you.

So before you can get a lead, produce a sale or make me happy, you must first prove you're a credible source. That way your prospects welcome your marketing message and believe what you say is different than the pitch-heavy communication they're force-fed every day.

Question #3: What is the most important aspect of any website?

    A. The content
    B. The design and layout
    C. The marketing message
    D. The strategy for driving traffic

Answer: D

You can have the most persuasive content, an award-winning design and a crystal-clear marketing message. But if your target prospects never see your website, then everything on it is essentially invisible.

Part I: Laying the Foundation for Effective Communication

Chapter #1

How Often Do You Use Marketing's Most Persuasive Word?

Before you get too far into this book, I encourage you to go through the following exercise to determine if your prospects — on a subconscious level — are tuning out your marketing message:

First, draw a line down the middle of a piece of paper. At the top of the left column, write the words "we" and "our" and then list your company name. At the top of the right column, write the words "you," "your" and "you're."

Next, find one of your marketing pieces. You may want to just pull up your website's home page.

Now read through your content sentence by sentence and place a mark in the left column whenever you come across the words "we," "our" or your company. Once you reach the bottom of the page, read the content again and put a mark in the right column each time you see the words "you," "your" or "you're."

What you'll likely notice first is a significant difference between the marks in both columns. In most cases, you'll have many more uses of the words from the left column than the ones in the right. In fact, you'll often see "we," "our" and your company name at the start of many sentences.

If the marks in your left column outnumber those in the right column, then you have a problem. Your prospects are likely ignoring your marketing message — often without realizing it because this action occurs on a subconscious level.

You see, your prospects are only concerned about themselves. When your content is filled with repeated uses of the words "we," "our" or your company name, you make your marketing message all about you.

This is like being that guy at a party who only talks about himself, laughs at his own jokes and always has a story that tops whatever anyone else says.

You've met this person before, right?

The easiest way to incorporate your prospects into your marketing message is to create content that reads more like a conversation and less like a corporate essay. When you use the words "you," "your" and "you're," you tell prospects your content is written specifically for them. Keep in mind the following study the next time you create content:

In an effort to determine what transforms unresponsive shoppers into enthusiastic buyers, researchers in the psychology department at Yale University studied consumers' reactions to certain words in advertisements. The results were compiled to create the 12 most persuasive words.

So what was the top word?

You. (In case you're interested, here are the others: money, save, new, results, health, easy, safety, love, discovery, proven and guarantee.)

Furthermore, "you" was listed as the most persuasive word in every marketing study performed by the researchers.

So don't wait to do this exercise. As you now know, "you" is a vital component to your marketing message.

Chapter #2

7 Overlooked Characteristics Shared by Prospects in All Industries

Many business owners and entrepreneurs turn to a common excuse when avoiding new marketing strategies.

The response is common when flawed prospect perceptions overshadow an opportunity for growth. In fact, you've probably heard the following phrase before (maybe even muttered it to yourself) ...

My prospects are different.

But the reality is all prospects share common characteristics, especially when deciding to part with their hard-earned cash. The only differences involve desires related to your product or service.

When marketing, your job is to establish trust in a way that proves you can deliver your prospects' desired outcome. Unfortunately, establishing trust these days is challenging, especially online. Lofty promises and fabricated facts get thrown around like rice at a wedding.

Fortunately, you can still cut through the marketing clutter by addressing these 7 characteristics shared by all prospects:

1. **Your prospects are skeptical.** How many times have you been disappointed with an outcome after a purchase? Maybe you were misled or the product or service didn't live up to its billing. Like you, your prospects have tossed away money on promises that

3

never panned out. Help them overcome skepticism by making frequent contact and delivering information they view as valuable.

Also, consider showing confidence in what you offer by giving a guarantee. Here's a portion of a great guarantee from A.G. Russell Knives:

> We guarantee total satisfaction. You, the customer, decide what satisfaction is. You decide how long you are entitled to be satisfied. If you buy a knife and don't use it for ten years and when you do use it you want to return it, do so. If you think that a knife should provide good service for ten years and it only does so for seven years, tell us so. You are in charge of our guarantee.

2. **Your prospects need direction.** As much as we want to view ourselves as leaders, our decisions are influenced by others, especially when we're in unfamiliar situations. Your prospects may have an idea about how to eliminate their problem (related to your product or service), but they desire your confirmation. So share your knowledge, give detailed instructions and allow them to see how you helped people in similar situations.

   "If-then" statements are one way to begin guiding prospects in your copy. Here's the formula: If (insert your prospect's problem(s) or desired result(s)), then (insert your bold promise or direction). Here's an example:

   > If you need to put your message in front of more prospects, then today's tip could be a game-changer for your marketing efforts.

3. **Your prospects don't want to feel alone.** People go to great lengths to avoid the fear of feeling physically or mentally isolated. That's why you must ensure your prospects believe their situation is not unique. But don't just tell them you understand their feelings — prove your desire to help by delivering solutions in your marketing.

You may even want to provide prospects with a place to exchange thoughts and receive support. Some businesses, such as WebMD, are built around this single concept.

4. **Your prospects dislike sales pitches.** When you feel purchase pressure, you naturally push back, right? If you allow your prospects to experience the same feeling, they'll direct attention elsewhere. Make your message welcome by educating, establishing credibility and involving your prospects in your marketing efforts.

   One way I like to slide under prospects' sales "radars" is through self-tests. Check out IKEA's online "Mattress guide" for an effective example. After answering a series of questions related to your sleeping habits, you get several mattress suggestions based on your responses.

   The benefit of self-tests is they allow prospects to reach conclusions themselves, which is more powerful than you pushing your own product or service.

5. **Your prospects' minds are flooded with marketing messages.** Dare to take a different approach. When you copy your competitors' marketing strategies, you instantly level the playing field. You may as well stop marketing altogether because it becomes impossible to secure space in your prospects' minds — you offer nothing on which they can base a buying a decision. A positive differentiation, however, can cause prospects to perceive your product or service as being better.

   Apple is often viewed as an obvious example of being different. The company doesn't try to be all things to all people. In fact, you could argue this factor makes Apple's products even more appealing to its target audience.

6. **Your prospects are afraid of the unknown.** Even if your marketing is so compelling it grabs eyeballs like glue, you risk missing out on responses unless you clearly communicate what happens after moving forward with your offer. What should your prospects expect? How will they feel? How will their situations change? Use

your marketing to help prospects visualize what it's like to work with you or use your product or service.

In recent promotions for Kindle Fire, Amazon.com uses two simple sentences to help prospects — especially anyone intimidated by technology — understand what to expect when the device shows up on their doorsteps:

Kindle Fire arrives preregistered to your Amazon.com account. So you're ready to go right out of the box.

7. **Your prospects have an internal buying clock.** You can't determine the time it takes your prospects to gather information, analyze the data and pull out their wallets — that decision is based on personal comfort. A common marketing mistake is trying to rush the process, resulting in unnecessary pressure. In some cases, however, you can impose deadlines and add incentives to speed up a sale.

When you create a sense of immediacy, your prospects realize they must respond now — or risk missing out on a valuable opportunity. The shopping rush on Black Friday is a perfect example of urgency in action. Once-a-year deals (sometimes only available for a few hours on that day) create a buying frenzy.

Chapter #3

Why Marketing Does Not Drive Profits

When do you make marketing a priority?

For many business owners and entrepreneurs, marketing only takes precedence when there's an immediate need for new leads.

And this presents a problem ...

You see, marketing because you're desperate for clients often creates a clouded perspective on the promotional process. Since you need profits, you scramble to find the easiest way to promote your product or service and, with any luck, get quick sales.

As a result, you're more likely to rely on a single idea — often the first one that comes to mind (or gets presented) — to pull you from the depths of despair.

Sound familiar? It does for me because I've fallen into this trap.

What makes matters worse is your marketing becomes more about what you offer and less about the prospects you target. So you promote what you need — not what your prospects want.

Before your marketing can drive profits, it must develop relationships.

Many business owners and entrepreneurs who launch marketing campaigns expect quick and significant returns. But those who consistently market realize campaigns take time, especially when you have to educate your target market.

Understand a single stab at a marketing strategy often isn't enough. Successful marketing relies on several well-planned strategies working together.

You also need consistency, which requires discipline. If at first nothing generates the results you desire, you must resolve to keep moving forward.

Fortunately, these days, the size of your company or marketing budget is no longer an advantage. Thanks to the Internet, you can compete and defeat larger competitors by simply producing a steady stream of quality information for your prospects.

If you don't regularly produce and share new content, you can start now. Simply engage your marketplace, find out what they want and then share your knowledge using the medium your prospects prefer.

Chapter #4

The Truth About How Your Occupation Affects Your Marketing

When it comes to effectively marketing your product or service, your prospects have little concern for your occupation.

They don't care if you're a lawyer ... real estate agent ... website developer ... auto mechanic ... bookkeeper ... doctor ... caterer ... whatever ...

Heck, I'm certain no one cares I'm a direct-response copywriter and marketing strategist. (You'll notice I rarely include this information in my marketing materials.)

Whether you're writing copy, coming up with lead-generating strategies or networking with other professionals, you share an occupation with every person who actively markets a business.

You're a problem solver.

The truth is purchasing decisions are not based on occupations ... or company names ... or logo designs ... or mission statements ... or the number of abbreviations after your name. Look around, however, and you see plenty of ego-based marketing messages focused on these items.

What wasted opportunities!

Prospects hunt for people who can solve their problems. The more your marketing message focuses on your prospects' nagging needs, the more often you'll receive responses. So showcase your expertise by offering information that details solutions.

There's no easier way to separate yourself from your competition.

Let me explain …

Imagine you want to sell your home and a real estate agent comes to your front door. She hands you a business card with the usual information (i.e., company name, agent's name, phone number, e-mail address and website) and tells you she sold many homes in your neighborhood. As she walks away, the agent encourages you to contact her when you're ready to list your house.

Shortly after the first agent leaves, another one shows up. Instead of a business card, she gives you a handout titled *5 Simple Strategies for Quickly Selling Your Home in a "Down" Market*. In addition to the tips, the guide includes specific examples and detailed testimonials of how homeowners in your neighborhood used the strategies to sell their properties. You also see several statements encouraging you to view the agent's website for more free tips.

Which website are you more likely to visit?

Which real estate agent established greater credibility?

Which real estate agent is more likely to get your business?

Chapter #5

How Well Do You Know Your Prospects' Problems?

Y ou already understand the importance of immediately capturing attention when persuading prospects to take action on your marketing materials.

After all, until you have eyeballs glued to your copy, anything you write is essentially invisible.

The way you attract attention comes down to two choices — you can write something your prospects know is true (but won't necessarily admit) or you can write something that worries them.

But here's the catch …

You can't write anything relevant unless you know your prospects' problems. **Before you sit in front of your keyboard or put pen to paper, you need a vivid picture of what keeps your target audience awake at night.**

Once you have this knowledge, you can create copy that speaks directly to them. What you write then becomes more believable because your message isn't just words on a page. Instead, it becomes a one-on-one conversation with a real human being.

The payoff comes when you zero in on something that resonates with a high percentage of your audience.

When I begin working with a new client, I use a questionnaire to help determine the copy's direction. The overall theme almost always comes from my fourth question:

What are your prospects' biggest concerns, emotions and needs? What information or help does he/she need to deal with them?

What I've discovered is most people don't do enough to learn about their prospects and customers. As a result, their copy becomes force-fed, self-serving information that offers little benefit to readers.

Your own e-mail list (which you should be actively building on your website) makes gathering knowledge about your prospects quick and easy. You can send out a survey and get direct feedback. Also, if you frequently communicate with your list and share knowledge, your subscribers will tell you what's causing them trouble.

Another option is my go-to tool for gathering insight about prospects — Amazon.com. When you visit the site, scan the reviews of popular books related to your industry. You'll find word-for-word explanations of your prospects' most pressing problems.

Chapter #6

7 Quick Ways to Eliminate Doubt from Your Marketing Copy

Your prospects become suspicious the instant they start reading your marketing materials.

The reaction is only natural. After all, when you're a prospect and you're asked to take action on an offer, your internal skeptic alarm goes off, too.

Right?

So you realize you only have a few seconds to reverse your prospects' thought process and get them on your side. The challenge is figuring out how to complete this transformation.

Here are seven quick ways to eliminate your prospects' doubt when they read your marketing copy:

1. **Address doubts immediately.** The longer you let suspicions linger, the more you risk your prospects fleeing to another marketing piece that better addresses their concerns. When you deal with objections, you become someone who helps rather than sells.

2. **Add personality.** Your copy isn't just words on a page. If you want interaction, you must view the words you write as a friendly

conversation. Prove to your prospects why you're just like them and you'll gain credibility.

3. **Write the way your prospects talk.** When you "speak" their language, you quickly establish a level of trust. Long words and jargon can create confusion and, in some cases, a sense of inadequacy.

4. **Support your claims with proof.** Testimonials, statistics and case studies go a long way in reducing doubt. Your prospects want to know people just like them were successful using your product or service.

5. **Encourage involvement.** Ask for opinions or responses to questions. Give prospects a checklist to help determine desires. You can even lead them to an audio, video or photo to engage their senses.

6. **Give an escape route.** This means making your offer risk-free. A guarantee or trial period shows confidence in what you offer and allows prospects to test your product or service on their own terms.

7. **Deliver value.** When you give freely, your prospects feel more inclined to return the favor. There's no substitute for making them feel like you truly care about their needs.

Keep in mind, regardless of how well you write your copy, you'll never get prospects to do anything they don't want to do. All you can do is capitalize on an unfilled need or desire.

Chapter #7

Which is More Important When Marketing — Your Message or Your Audience?

I f you had to pick between delivering a powerful marketing message to a large audience of people or selecting a small group of *prospects* to receive a poor marketing message, which would you choose?

My answer might surprise you …

I'll take the small group of prospects and poor marketing message almost every time.

After all, when put in front of the wrong audience, even the most persuasive marketing messages get ignored. Of course, this fact goes against advice you often hear from sales trainers.

Many say you should play the "numbers game." Get in front of more people and you'll get more sales.

Sure, there's some truth to this claim. But marketing to people who haven't expressed interest in what you offer drains resources.

Remember, you can't create desire where none exists — you can only deepen a desire that's already present. Trying to convince people they need your product or service will only leave you frustrated and your wallet thinner.

Buying an ad in your local newspaper or magazine because you want your message in front of thousands of eyeballs doesn't guarantee marketing success.

Neither does posting a banner on a highly trafficked website ... mailing to large lists of nearby homes or businesses ... growing a huge following on social media ... securing a full-page spread in the Yellow Pages ... or even buying a commercial spot during the Super Bowl.

The list could go on.

Before you roll out a major campaign, make sure the marketing medium you use reaches an audience that already expressed desire for your offer. You'll be in even better shape if those same people already purchased a similar product or service.

Let me explain ...

Imagine you're a Chicago ticket broker with access to seats for pretty much any sporting event.

This season happens to be the year my beloved Chicago Cubs break the curse and play in the World Series. We've now reached Game 7 and my loveable losers are hosting the final game at Wrigley Field.

As a life-long Cubs fan, I try every trick possible to get two tickets to the game — but I'm unsuccessful. However, I decide to fly to Chicago, show up at the ballpark and take my chances at snagging a pair of seats.

You (being the smart marketer you are) realize many fans share my situation. So you also show up at Wrigley Field to sell tickets.

Within seconds of stepping out your car, you see me holding a flimsy cardboard sign expressing my desire to get inside the ballpark. So you walk over and show me two tickets.

Do you think a powerful marketing message is necessary to persuade me to buy your seats?

No way!

Even if you don't mutter a word, will I still want your tickets?

Of course!

Now imagine you have those same Cubs tickets, but this time you show up 1,751 miles away at Sun Devil Stadium. The Arizona State Sun Devils (my alma mater) are hosting the University of Arizona Wildcats, arguably the biggest football game of the year in Arizona.

Nearly 74,000 people are expected. So you set up outside the stadium entrance and begin promoting your Cubs tickets.

Even though hoards of sports fans are expected to file past you, is it likely you'll get buyers?

Probably not.

But what if you have an incredibly persuasive marketing message? After all, Sun Devil Stadium's capacity is nearly twice that of Wrigley Field. So you can reach about 33,000 more fans, many who probably enjoy baseball, too.

Obviously, even with the larger audience, the likelihood of a sale is slim.

Make sense?

Part II. **Building a Bond and Creating Trust**

Chapter #8

Don't Fall for Marketing's Most Hyped Desire

Take a guess at when the following quote was said …

"Advertisements are now so numerous that they are very negligently perused, and it is therefore become necessary to gain attention by magnificence of promises, and by eloquence sometimes sublime and sometimes pathetic."

I saw this statement while reading John Morgan's bestseller, *Brand Against the Machine: How to Build Your Brand, Cut Through the Marketing Noise, and Stand Out from the Competition.* At first glance, you might think the quote was pulled from a current business journal, trade publication or maybe an online blog post.

But it was written by English author Samuel Johnson, who penned his theory in the January 20, 1759, edition of *The Idler.*

Crazy, isn't it?

It's been 253 years and Johnson's words still ring true.

Many business owners and entrepreneurs continue force-feeding promotional messages as if their product or service is the only game in town. They push pitch after pitch with little concern for people's fading attention spans.

What's often overlooked is attention alone doesn't create sales. If getting noticed was all you needed to build a business, you could create a Fortune 500 company from scratch by simply shelling out millions for a 30-second Super Bowl spot.

The most critical piece in the promotional puzzle is trust.

That's why marketing is no longer about you or your company. Today's marketing is about interacting and delivering value to those who need your help.

Remember, the currency in today's marketing world is information — not money. As you share more information, your status as an authority soars.

Dr. Mehmet Oz is an incredible marketer. Thanks to the information he shares, the cardiothoracic surgeon moves products at a staggering pace. Watch *The Dr. Oz Show* and you'll see him offer advice about pressing health issues, including problems many people won't discuss with their own doctors.

He also publishes books, writes for magazines and newspapers, and hosts radio shows.

On his website, you'll find how-to articles, videos and quizzes on topics such as deadly drug interactions, fighting fatigue, fixing infections, overcoming the flu and battling weight issues. Dr. Oz is truly the go-to source for health information because his content has created trust with millions of consumers.

Imagine you had an ailment requiring an operation. Would you feel comfortable if Dr. Oz was the surgeon holding the scalpel?

I bet you would.

Chapter #9

The Trend That Will Drive Marketing Success for at Least the Next Decade

You may have noticed …

The change in the marketing game means no longer are mega companies with big budgets at an advantage.

In today's marketing world, you — as a small business owner and entrepreneur — have the edge because successful strategies are no longer defined by the depths of your pockets.

The Internet has leveled the playing field.

If you want to get into the marketing game today, you simply have to step off the sidelines. A growing collection of free tools are available to you right now.

For example, you can create a TV channel, start a radio program or syndicate your content to a worldwide audience without leaving the comfort of your office chair.

Just a few years ago, these options were only available to heavy hitters who could afford to buy the equipment and hire the knowledge needed to reach a mass audience.

Today, not only can you experiment with text, video and audio without worrying about blowing your budget, but you maintain complete control over your marketing message.

If you want to make the most of this opportunity, then it's important you understand what you're about to read next ...

First, keep in mind, more people than ever turn to the Internet for information. What they're looking for are solutions or entertainment.

Not all that long ago, people just consumed the information they found. Now, they often take an additional step — one that can quickly propel your marketing message.

They share.

If you produce useful information that addresses your prospects' problems, it will get in front of eyeballs. Thanks to the explosion of social media sites such as Facebook, LinkedIn and Twitter (as well as easy accessibility to e-mail), sharing articles, videos and pictures is a regular activity for many people.

So how "shareable" is your current content? Are you putting out useful information for your prospects — or is your marketing message focused on you and your company?

When you consistently deliver valuable content, you establish yourself a trusted authority. Then, as others share your marketing message, your influence grows stronger.

Chapter #10

The 2 Most Critical Elements in a Marketing Relationship

How you're perceived when marketing to your prospects comes down to two factors.

Neither one has anything to do with experience ... schooling ... years in business ... location ... skill level ... budget ... or technical knowledge.

Instead, the two most critical elements in a marketing relationship are the frequency of your interaction and the value of your communication.

Simply put, you must contact your prospects often and give them information they view as valuable.

Think of the courtship process in marketing as being similar to your relationship with your spouse or significant other. It's safe to assume the connection you have now isn't the same as when you met the first time.

Your relationship took time to develop, right?

In the case of a marketing campaign, the common mistake it trying to rush the relationship by initiating contact only when you have something to sell.

Can you imagine the relationship you'd have with your spouse or significant other if the only time you talked to him/her was when you sought out personal gain? You don't have to be Dr. Phil to realize your "relationship" would sour quickly.

The reality is people are more likely to buy from you after you've gained their trust and established a relationship — outcomes that require time and frequent contact.

Make sense?

The bottom line is you must prove to your prospects you care about their needs before you'll have any success pitching your product or service.

Chapter #11

What Your Financial Planner Can Teach You About Reducing Marketing Risk

T he other day, while writing print ads for two side projects, I was reminded of a common marketing mistake.

And I must admit, I'm as guilty of this oversight as anyone.

You see, when it comes to marketing my business, I have a system that helps generate leads on a pretty consistent basis. Unfortunately, this marketing method is so ingrained in my brain that I often overlook other opportunities.

To put my admission bluntly ...

There are times when my personal marketing lacks diversification.

I often have to remind myself just how many cost-effective marketing methods are available today.

Promotional activities for my own business are primarily directed toward online tactics. But I've learned over the years my target audience doesn't only look for solutions on the Internet. They gather information from a variety of sources.

Your target audience likely shares this same characteristic. After all, most people need a combination of interactions with a brand before they even consider prying open their wallets.

Like any smart financial investment, effective marketing entails spreading out your risk. But you can't stop there — you also have to measure your returns.

Unfortunately, some marketing mediums produce a more defined response than others.

For example, campaigns with print, TV or radio ads allow you to judge response by incorporating a promotional code, designated phone number or unique URL into the call to action. And, if you offer a free report or other giveaway on your website (which you should), you can easily track the percentage of visitors who request that information.

On the other hand, social media activities are tougher to measure, especially on a monetary level. But you can still track objectives such as mentions, fans and page views.

So how are you diversifying and measuring your marketing efforts?

Chapter #12

6 Words That Will Make You a Marketing Superstar

Imagine asking a room full of business owners and entrepreneurs for their definitions of marketing.

You'd probably hear several words repeated, such as "sales," "selling" and "promoting." But it's likely many would miss mentioning a critical piece in the marketing process — something you need before anyone considers spending a single cent with you.

Trust.

That's why I came up with the following definition:

Marketing is the process of establishing trust in a way that proves you can deliver your prospects' desired outcome.

You see, as mentioned earlier, marketing involves initiating and developing relationships similar to the one you have with a spouse. The most important component to both interactions is trust.

But, as you know, trust takes time.

These days, establishing trust with prospects and even your own clients is challenging, especially online. Lofty promises and fabricated facts get tossed around like rumors at a high school.

But you can still cut through the chaos. In fact, the easiest way is to focus your marketing on the following six-word question:

What do my prospects want most?

Now, before jumping to conclusions, let me remind you of a fact that might sound a little harsh …

Prospects don't want your product or service. Believing they do only leads to frustration and unsuccessful marketing campaigns.

What prospects want is the *outcome* delivered by your product or service.

Understand the difference?

So if you're a portrait photographer, your prospects don't want you to take pictures — they want visual memories they can't wait to share with friends and family. If you're a criminal defense lawyer, a guy just pulled over for extreme DUI doesn't want legal representation — he wants to stay out of jail, get his record cleared and have a chance at living a normal life again.

Your marketing must provide insight that puts prospects closer to their desired outcome.

Recently, I was introduced to a passage from Wallace D. Wattles' 1910 classic, *The Science of Getting Rich.* Many view the book as the basis for most personal finance and self-help literature written today.

Check out how Wattles describes our natural desire for knowledge and understanding — as if they're internal forces you can't turn off:

In so far as your business consists in dealing with other men, whether personally or by the letter, the key thought of all your efforts must be to convey to their minds the impression of increase.

Increase is what all men and all women are seeking. It is the urge of the Formless Intelligence within them, seeking fuller expression.

The desire for increase is inherent in all nature; it is the fundamental impulse of the universe. All human activities are based on the desire for increase. People are seeking more food, more clothes, better shelter, more luxury, more beauty, more knowledge, more pleasure — increase in something — more life.

Every living thing is under the necessity for continuous advancement. Where increase in life ceases, dissolution and death set in at once.

Man instinctively knows this, and hence he is forever seeking more.

So what's the "more" your prospects ask for?

Chapter #13

How to Match Your Marketing With What Your Prospects Want

Here's a quick tip for the next time you need to create copy that connects with your prospects and makes them eager for what you offer ...

This piece in the persuasion process is one you can't overlook because it helps prove to prospects you understand their situation. As a result, you get viewed more as a helpful friend than a sly salesman.

So here the tip ...

Before you begin writing, you need a clear understanding of your prospects' thoughts. Or, as renowned copywriter Robert Collier stated in *The Robert Collier Letter Book*, you must "enter the conversation that's already going on in your prospect's mind."

You see, once you understand your prospects' frustrations, beliefs and desires, your copy can explain how your offering bridges the gap between where they are today and where they want to be.

Make sense?

Now, before we go any further, let get clear about something else.

Your prospects' primary concern is not your goals, your mission or your company's history. They also have little concern with what you want to sell them.

What your prospects want to know is how you can help them solve their problem(s). Fortunately for you, these issues are often at the forefront of their thought process.

One way to match your marketing with what's in your prospects' minds is to simply survey them. If you're actively building a prospect list using your website and other marketing mediums (which, again, you should), then ask your subscribers about their most pressing issues related to your product or service. If you have a targeted list, you'll find several shared frustrations.

Another mind-matching marketing technique is to tap into current events. For example, as I write this chapter, news about the tornado that ripped through Joplin, Missouri, dominates most media. Is there a way you can apply this tragedy to your marketing?

Or, is there an upcoming holiday you can work into your next promotion? What about a celebrity making news?

And, finally, your website analytics act in a similar manner to a survey when determining what your prospects want. If your website delivers value to visitors through frequently updated, educational content, begin monitoring the keywords and phrases visitors use to land on your pages. Before long, you'll notice trends you can use to create more content and solutions for your prospects.

Chapter #14

Have You Addressed the Internal Fear Found in All Prospects?

Your prospects have an internal fear that, if not addressed in your marketing, is almost certainly causing you to lose leads.

This fear sits at the core of human nature, having a major effect on how we respond to nearly every situation. In extreme cases, the concern becomes so great it causes panic attacks.

So what is it?

Being alone.

No one wants to feel physically or mentally isolated. That's why it's critical your prospects believe what they're going through is not unique.

As crazy as it seems, simply including the words "you're not alone" in your marketing materials can create a connection. (In fact, some marketers claim a "You're not alone" e-mail subject line results in strong open rates.)

But don't rely on just telling prospects you understand their feelings — prove your desire to help them. Begin by delivering solutions in your marketing.

For example, what questions do you hear over and over again from prospects? Make these responses readily available and encourage interaction.

How many times have you been in unfamiliar surroundings and hesitated to ask a question? Maybe you believed you were the only person with that issue ... were afraid of the response ... or feared what other people would think about you.

These situations happen all the time, right? So why allow your prospects to share these same feelings?

At an absolute minimum, guide them through the most common mistakes related to your product or service.

Also, what thoughts go through your prospects' minds while searching for your product or service? If you don't address these beliefs, they'll likely create false ideas about your offer.

And, finally, don't forget testimonials. Remember, knowing someone else went through the same experience as you — and had a successful outcome — is comforting. Proof elements such as testimonials also allow you to tap into prospects' natural tendency to react in a similar manner to people who are just like them.

Chapter #15

The Enviable Marketing Position That's Yours for the Taking

Legendary copywriter Gary Bencivenga recommends the ultimate barometer for testing any marketing piece.

While his suggestion specifically focuses on advertising, there's little chance your responses won't improve when you apply it to your marketing materials. The truth is, however, few people will dedicate the effort required to create promotional pieces that meet the high standard Bencivenga suggests.

This is good news for you because it presents an incredible opportunity.

But before I explain why, here's Bencivenga's advice:

Make your advertising too valuable to throw away.

The concept is simple, but the execution is anything but easy.

You see, too often marketing is viewed as a repetitive practice of placing logos, product descriptions and prices, facts about services, and contact information in as many locations as possible — actions that rely on blind luck and do little to address what prospects truly want.

To make your marketing materials valuable, you must create exceptional content. Fortunately, you have the ability to deliver unlimited value to your prospects by giving them information that helps address their problems related to your product or service.

In turn, each time you share your knowledge, you further establish yourself as an authority in your industry. And wouldn't you agree people prefer working with experts they know, like and trust?

So don't wait around for someone to designate you an expert. Grab that title today — it's your position!

You don't need a large audience ... you don't need a big budget ... you don't need any special equipment or training ...

You just need the guts to give advice (even better if in a public setting), share what you know and demonstrate why you are an authority.

Remember, each time you start writing a marketing piece, you begin with a blank document — a virtual piece of paper that's worthless.

However, as you add words, the value increases based on the knowledge you share. The more you reveal, the greater the value.

Chapter #16

An Easy Way to Create Credibility When Marketing to Skeptical Prospects

Although earning credibility takes times, you can shortcut the process.

Whether you're a seasoned industry veteran or an absolute newbie, the strategy you're about to learn will expand your exposure, give you valuable content and boost your celebrity status. But I must warn you …

Most people who know this strategy never use it because they're afraid of rejection. In some cases, they're also scared of sharing the spotlight.

So what is it?

Interviewing experts in your industry.

You simply ask a series of questions, record your conversation and then distribute the information. Seems pretty simple, right?

It is.

If you follow my personal marketing, you know this strategy is one of my favorites.

You see, you put the power of association at play when you interview experts. You're perceived as an authority because you associate

39

with industry leaders. You also gain an advantage because you get top-notch advice for free.

How cool is that?

When you interview people, they often share their most valuable knowledge because they don't want to look bad. Also, your interviewees will often tell their audiences about your discussion. As a result, your work gets introduced to potential prospects nearly every time you conduct an interview.

(And be prepared. Once you start distributing your recordings and/ or transcripts, you'll get your own interview requests.)

The biggest challenge you face is the courage to ask for interviews. However, you'd be surprised at how many people give their time if you just ask them. So don't let fear of rejection stop you.

Of course, your chances for approval increase when you request interviews with people you know. If your contacts aren't well-known experts to your target audience, don't worry. The information shared during your interviews is more important than your sources.

Unique insight often comes from lesser-known people. Furthermore, sometimes knowledge shared by well-known figures gets repeated so often that it no longer packs a punch.

Another potential stumbling block is creating questions for your interviews. You can overcome this challenge with a little brainstorming. If you were in an audience listening to your interviewee, what questions would you want answered?

When I'm stumped for questions, I turn to Amazon.com. Spend a few minutes scanning the table of contents in books related to your interview topic and you'll find more question material than you can handle.

Okay, so now let's talk equipment ...

You can conduct your interviews by phone or online video. I prefer phone interviews because they're easier to edit, distribute and store. Furthermore, people can upload the files and listen to them away from their computers.

Regardless of format, consider transcribing your interviews. That way people who prefer reading over listening can still consume your content. (If you need a transcriptionist, I recommend Deborah Wallis at One on One Transcription: http://www.oneononetranscription.com.)

You can begin conducting your interviews without buying any equipment. A service such as FreeConferenceCall.com will record your call when you set up an account and use one of their phone numbers. I use my land line and a Voice Path™ device from JK Audio (about $100). The small box has three cables that route my phone's audio to my computer's sound card.

I then use software to record, edit and play back the conversation. I prefer Sony's Sound Forge Audio Studio. For Mac users, I hear GarageBand is an excellent option. If you want free services, search online for options such as Audacity.

For in-person interviews and online podcasts, save yourself future frustrations and invest in a quality microphone. For whatever it's worth, my microphone is an M-Audio Producer USB.

Obviously, I'm comfortable using these tools — and you may find better equipment. The key is not letting a piece of equipment prevent you from taking action on this strategy. You can do your first interview today.

And one final point …

Any interview you record is a potential information product. Yes, you can sell your interviews and even bundle several together to create a larger product.

Now who do you want to interview?

Chapter #17

Are You Giving Away Too Much Information?

Time to tackle the most common question I get from prospects and clients.

As you know by now, I recommend sharing knowledge that helps your prospects address problems related to your product or service. Although I prefer using special reports, you can use this sharing strategy with all types of media, including audio and video.

Regardless of the format, there's really no better way to attract prospects.

But I understand why some people hesitate to give away their knowledge. They believe sharing what you know leads prospects to solve problems themselves, without needing your product or service.

But this belief is far from reality.

I'll explain why. But first, let's get into the most common question ...

If you share information, how do you know when you've given away too much?

Honestly, I don't worry about this "problem." **You see, when you share your knowledge, you make your marketing all about your**

prospects. This step alone puts you in a stronger position than your competitors whose marketing only focuses on their own desires.

Also, sharing information is a lot like cooking from a recipe. For example, imagine Bobby Flay and I get the same step-by-step instructions on how to grill filet mignon with a balsamic glaze. Even if we both have identical grills, ingredients and tools, do you think we'd end up with the same result?

Of course not!

Bobby is a grilling expert, while I'm a novice who can only hope to create a meal my kids will eat without much fuss.

The information you share with prospects is supported by experience that comes from applying your product or service to your business every day. You could deliver exact instructions to your prospects on how to solve their problem, but there's little chance they'll end up with the same outcome as you.

Another advantage of sharing knowledge is the time savings. You don't waste hours repeating answers to the same questions. What's more, your message reaches a wider audience. After all, there are only so many people you can talk to in a day.

And that's not all …

When prospects read your information, they instantly recognize you an expert on your topic.

Remember, prospects won't hire you or buy your product unless they understand what you can do for them. So when you share your knowledge, you help establish credibility and trust, while proving you can help your prospects.

Part III: **Crafting Your Marketing Message**

Chapter #18

Do You Dare to Be Different With Your Marketing Message?

S uccessful marketing requires attracting attention to your business. Wouldn't you agree?

Fortunately, you have an advantage because you're different than your competitors — you have unique characteristics. In some cases, these traits may naturally help you or your business stand out ... and that's a good thing.

After all, there's a strong chance you market to the same prospects as your competitors.

Realize marketing without making an effort to be different is bad. Copying your competitors' strategies levels the playing field. As such, you may as well stop marketing altogether because it becomes impossible to secure space in your prospects' minds — you offer nothing on which they can base a buying decision.

A positive differentiation, however, causes your prospects to perceive your product or service as being better.

Duplicating marketing strategies is common in all industries. For proof, open your newspaper and look at the ads for car dealers ... flip through your phone book and check out the dentist listings ... look through the letters in your mailbox from cable television or dish providers and review their offers … enter a keyword from your industry in a search engine and review some websites …

You'll notice many marketing pieces share a common look and similar content. For example, how many times have you seen companies promote excellent customer service or tout having the best product?

Boring!

To be different, you must try new approaches and take measured risks.

So how can you do things differently with your marketing message? Here are two quick suggestions:

- **Encourage interaction.** One of my favorite ways to get prospects involved is through self-tests. For an example of this technique, check out the quick quiz at the beginning of this book.

- **Take ideas from other industries.** Frankly, any marketing techniques you repeatedly see in your industry are likely tired and worn out. But you'll find new offers and ways to position your product or service when you study marketing materials from other industries.

Chapter #19

Which of These Desires Turns Your Prospects Into Buyers?

I f you want to get greater responses from your marketing materials without spending more money, here's a fact you must remember: **You can't create desire where none exists — you can only deepen a desire that's already present.**

Trying to convince people they need your product or service puts you in an impossible position for marketing success.

Remember, every person is not your prospect.

The most cost-effective marketing involves targeting people who have expressed interest in what you offer (or something similar).

This is one reason why a two-step marketing approach works well, especially for high-priced products and services.

The first step delivers a no-risk sample of your offering, while allowing prospects to qualify themselves. The second step — which is more of a process — involves developing relationships so you can better match your prospects' buying preferences.

Fortunately, there are several desires shared by just about everyone. About three years ago when I interviewed advertising consultant and trainer Drew Eric Whitman, author or *Cashvertising: How to Use More than 100 Secrets of Ad-Agency Psychology to Make Big Money Sell-*

ing Anything to Anyone, he revealed what he calls his "Life-Force 8" — eight biologically programmed desires shared by most human beings. Here's his list:

1. Survival, the enjoyment of life and life extension
2. Enjoyment of food and beverages
3. Freedom from pain, fear and danger
4. Sexual companionship
5. Comfortable living conditions
6. To be superior
7. Care and protection of loved ones
8. Social approval

Once you identify one of these desires fulfilled by your product or service, simply prove to prospects your offer delivers that sought-after outcome.

Chapter #20

A Simple Way to Avoid Creating Confusion With Your Marketing Message

A common misconception causes confusion and drives prospects away from your marketing materials. Unfortunately, this problem has broadened as more business owners and professionals write their own promotional copy.

A common belief in business is that using long, complex words and phrases in marketing materials is an effective way to demonstrate knowledge. The implication is that if your sentences are short and simple, prospects won't view you as credible — or, worse yet, educated.

But the reality is your prospects seek simplicity. By using everyday words and phrases, you make your marketing message easier to understand.

Here's why ...

You must remember your mind thinks in pictures. When you read (or hear) words or phrases, your brain uses past experiences to subconsciously create what are basically mental movies. Simple words produce images that are easy to understand and remember.

But their complex counterparts cause your brain to work harder. As a result, mental images become unclear because you have fewer experiences to associate with the words or phrases.

And here's another problem ...

Complex words and phrases can trigger indecision because some prospects will feel like you're trying to hide something. And if that's not troublesome enough, you also increase the risk offending your readers.

So as a general rule, avoid using a long word when a short one will do.

Chapter #21

A 3-Step Approach for Adding Emotional Appeal to Your Marketing Materials

If you regularly market your business, you know you can't just put facts about your product or service in front of anyone and get a strong response.

Facts alone rarely offer enough information to trigger action.

Responses require copy that speaks directly to targeted prospects on an emotional level because emotions serve as the foundation for all buying decisions.

Here are three steps to help you write copy that appeals to your prospects' internal senses:

Step 1: Call out your prospects by stating the problem you can help them solve.

The benefit of pinpointing a problem is it allows you to zero in on thoughts already in your prospects' minds. After all, when an issue causes you stress, you can't stop thinking about it, right?

And, because your prospects are already pondering a problem, it's easier to bypass the brain's natural reaction to reject new ideas.

Step 2: Address beliefs your prospects have about their problem.

Common thoughts shape your prospects' attitudes about the solution you offer. They may believe your solution is too expensive ... you don't have enough experience ... you're too busy to help ... you'll pressure them with a sales pitch at the first opportunity ...

As for their problem, maybe they believe it's too complicated for a quick solution ... requires resources they can't access ... involves issues no one else has experienced ... entails dealing with topics they're too embarrassed to discuss ...

Whatever their beliefs, you must address these concerns or you risk losing your prospects' attention.

Step 3: Figure out how your prospects feel.

Are they frustrated, scared or confused? Do they feel guilty? Are they insecure about their situation?

Once you know these answers, add to your marketing materials the exact words your prospects use to describe their feelings. Taking this step helps prove to your prospects you understand them because you "speak" their language.

Chapter #22

Try This Writing Formula on Your Next Marketing Piece

If predicting the location of NASA's falling satellite debris in 2011 proved easier than writing your last marketing piece, then the formula you'll soon see should solve your struggles.

But before revealing the process, understand I take zero credit for this tip. The recognition goes to Bob Bly, a renowned copywriter and author of several best-selling books on copywriting and marketing. (Yep, even Bly's freebies at http://www.bly.com are outstanding.)

Recently, I heard Bly on an e-mail marketing webinar explain his "motivating sequence" for persuading people through copy. The following is his formula (and my explanations for each step):

1. **Get attention.** Anything you mention in your marketing piece is essentially invisible unless you first gain your prospects' awareness. Try piquing curiosity with a question, tying your headline into current news, stating an alarming statistic or making a bold statement.

2. **Identify the problem or need.** Regardless of target audience, your product or service addresses an issue facing your prospects. So once you have their attention, remind them of the problem(s).

Also, consider agitating the problem by explaining how putting it off can create additional challenges.

3. **Position your product or service as the solution to your prospects' problem.** This step is often forced too early in the persuasion process. As a result, the marketing message ignores prospects and instead describes the greatness surrounding a company's product or service.

4. **Provide proof.** Without evidence, solutions become empty words stealing space in your marketing materials. Remember, your prospects are skeptical. Show them you're credible and prove what you offer is legit by incorporating testimonials, case studies, references to research, comparisons or a guarantee.

5. **Ask for action.** Many opportunities get missed on marketing materials because prospects don't know how to respond. So make the next step crystal clear. And, whether you want an inquiry or an order, tell prospects how they get rewarded when taking action.

Chapter #23

Can You Really Trigger a Buying Trance With Your Marketing Message?

Imagine having an almost magical power that allows you to put prospects into a positive mental state relating to your product or service.

You might be surprised to know this skill is obtainable. In fact, triggering a buying trance with your written words isn't as complicated as you might think.

Success comes down to your ability to attract targeted prospects. Because once you have these people's interest, you can shape their mental imagery and lead them down a path to your desired outcome.

Unfortunately, you face a dominant obstacle — the mind's natural defense mechanism.

You see, your mind doesn't welcome change. As a result, instant rejection is much more common than acceptance. This decision process occurs instantly and often without conscious control.

The moment your marketing message contains an idea your prospects' minds can't accept, any thought of making a purchase is rejected and your opportunity is lost forever. But when you can switch off the brain's critical component, you give your marketing message a fighting chance of getting evaluated.

One way to temporarily disable your prospects' inner critic is by calling attention to specific problems. After all, problems are "messages" your mind can relate to because you're actively thinking about them.

Here's an example …

When promoting one of my special reports, *Marketing Materials Made Easy: 8 Secrets for Attracting Attention, Creating Customers and Building Your Business*, I target certain prospects with the following phrase:

For business owners and professionals fed up by the lack of leads generated by their company's marketing materials — and can't figure out what's wrong …

Notice how I don't just target "business owners" or "professionals." What good would it do me to pursue such a general group?

Instead, I want business owners and professionals who are concerned about their marketing materials … frustrated because their promotional efforts are failing … and confused about what can be done to generate leads. Once I have the attention of these targeted prospects, I can then pile on the reasons for needing my special report.

You can use this same approach in any industry.

Let's say you're a criminal defense lawyer in Chicago. Here's a possible statement:

For Chicago residents accused of a violent crime who feel overwhelmed with decisions, confused about legal options and scared about their future — and can't figure out where to turn for honest advice …

Pretty simple strategy, isn't it?

Chapter #24

A Copywriting Cure for Boring Marketing Materials

Boredom.

It's the demise of all marketing materials.

If you can't instantly grab your prospects' attention, any piece you use to promote your business becomes invisible. This is one reason why a strong headline is essential.

But once prospects read past your headline, you still must keep them interested. You also want to make them active participants in your marketing message.

The following copywriting strategy is one way you can maintain your prospects' attention and keep them engaged. What makes this approach so powerful is your copy gets readers to realize they need your product or service. Best of all, they come to this conclusion without you actually telling them.

Here's how it works ...

After you write your headline, begin your body copy with a series of questions. The secret to this strategy is the answers to these questions.

Your prospects should only know the answers if they have the knowledge to achieve their desired end result. If they don't know the answers, then your product or service becomes the logical solution to their problems.

The easiest way to understand this strategy is with an example. So take a minute to read the following squeeze page copy I recently wrote targeting Canadian consumers shopping for a mortgage:

Do you know how to lock in the guaranteed lowest interest rate on your mortgage (for as long as 120 days) — even before you begin shopping for your next home?

Do you know what time of the year offers the best opportunity for buying property at a discount?

If you have bruised credit or a bankruptcy, do you know the steps you must take to prove you can manage your money and how to then find lenders who will eagerly give you low interest rates?

As you know, today's economy has changed the rules for lending. But that doesn't mean you still can't save thousands of dollars on your mortgage or refinance.

The problem you face is confusion. With so many changes, it's nearly impossible to stay on top of all the programs and pitfalls facing today's consumers. It's no wonder why so many people have given up on getting their dream homes.

If the lending process has left you more confused than empowered, take a deep breath and relax. You're about to get an entirely new outlook on how you can secure a hassle-free home mortgage.

Notice how the questions point out to prospects their lack of information. The only way to get the knowledge they need is by requesting the free special report I wrote for the client as a lead-capture tool. The instant a report is requested, the client knows that prospect needs a mortgage.

Pretty painless way to get qualified leads, isn't it?

Here's another example of the same copywriting strategy used in an article I wrote about hiring effective employees:

Do you know why you instantly eliminate up to 90 percent of available job candidates when you limit your search to temporary workers?

If your firm struggles with efficiency or redundancy, do you know why immediately filling your full-time vacancy with a full-time employee can cause you to squander time and money?

Do you know why you should avoid sharing your company, department and job role needs before questioning candidates during your interviews?

These are innocent mistakes that nearly everyone makes when filling vacant positions. But with some simple knowledge, you'll have no problem avoiding them the next time you hire new staff.

In this case, prospects must continue reading the article to find out the answers.

In both examples, did you notice there are no "me" messages (i.e., messages about a company or individual)? Instead, all the copy appeals to a prospect's needs and wants.

Chapter #25

How to Craft a Unique Advertising Message for a Common Product or Service

About 80 years ago, Claude Hopkins had a problem you probably faced at some point during your business career.

The advertising writer had just landed a campaign with a struggling company. But the fact that the company had trouble attracting the customers they wanted was only a minor issue.

The primary problem was the product — it was anything but unique. Several companies shared what essentially was an identical product. In fact, the product was so common that it was already in homes and taverns throughout the United States.

The new client was Schlitz and the product was beer.

At the time, Schlitz held fifth place in its industry. The strategy you're about to read propelled the Milwaukee brewer into a tie for first after only a few months.

Schlitz's rise to prominence has been called the greatest success in beer advertising. Not only do you see beer's biggest brands using the same strategy today, but it's also something you can apply to any business.

When Hopkins began studying other beer companies, he noticed they all announced the same claim in their advertising — "pure." In his book, *My Life in Advertising*, Hopkins explained how brewers would publicize the word in big letters. Some would even buy double-page ads so "pure" was displayed as large as possible.

Hopkins recognized the claim had little effect on prospects. So he went to a Schlitz brewery in search of a solution ...

Once there, he saw plate-glass rooms filled with filtered air where beer dripped over pipes. The process allowed the beer to cool in purity.

Next, he saw large filters packed with white-wood pulp, and then watched how every pump and pipe was cleaned twice daily to avoid contamination. Even the bottles were washed four times by machinery.

Although the brewery sat on the shores of Lake Michigan, Hopkins saw how Schlitz tapped artesian wells to collect pure water from 4,000 feet below the ground. He was also shown vats where beer aged for six months before it went to users.

A stop in the laboratory revealed how the yeast used in Schlitz beer was developed from an original cell that required 1,200 experiments before the finest taste was discovered.

Once back at the office, Hopkins asked, "Why don't you tell people these things? Why do you merely try to cry louder than others that your beer is pure? Why don't you tell the reasons?"

"Why?" was the response. "The processes we use are just the same as others use. No one can make good beer without them."

Hopkins had a hunch people would respond to reading how Schlitz achieved "pure" beer. So he used print ads to tell stories that gave purity meaning.

Here are a couple of those ads:

In Filtered Air.

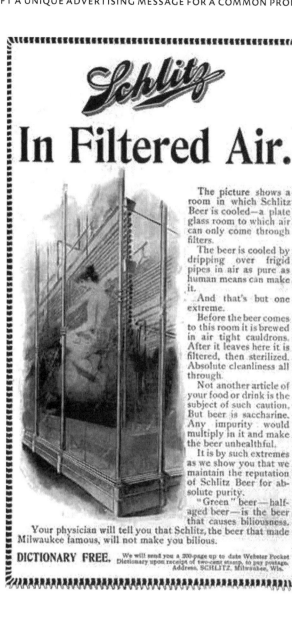

The picture shows a room in which Schlitz Beer is cooled—a plate glass room to which air can only come through filters.

The beer is cooled by dripping over frigid pipes in air as pure as human means can make it.

And that's but one extreme.

Before the beer comes to this room it is brewed in air tight cauldrons. After it leaves here it is filtered, then sterilized. Absolute cleanliness all through.

Not another article of your food or drink is the subject of such caution. But beer is saccharine. Any impurity would multiply in it and make the beer unhealthful.

It is by such extremes as we show you that we maintain the reputation of Schlitz Beer for absolute purity.

"Green" beer—half-aged beer—is the beer that causes biliousness. Your physician will tell you that Schlitz, the beer that made Milwaukee famous, will not make you bilious.

DICTIONARY FREE. We will send you a 200-page up to date Webster Pocket Dictionary upon receipt of two-cent stamp, to pay postage. Address, SCHLITZ, Milwaukee, Wis.

Perfection of 50 Years

Back of each glass of Schlitz Beer there is an experience of fifty years.

In 1848, in a hut, Joseph Schlitz began brewing. Not beer like Schlitz beer of today; but it was honest. It was the best beer an American had ever brewed.

This great brewery today has new methods. A half century has taught us perfection. But our principles are 50 years old; our aims are unaltered. Schlitz beer is still brewed, without regard to expense, according to the best that we know.

We send experts to Bohemia to select for us the best hops in the world.

An owner of the business selects the barley, and buys only the best that grows.

A partner in our concern supervises every stage of the brewing.

Cleanliness is not carried to greater extremes in any kitchen than here.

Purity is made imperative. All beer is cooled in plate glass rooms, in filtered air. Then the beer is filtered. Then it is sterilized, after being bottled and sealed.

We age beer for months in refrigerating rooms before it goes out. Otherwise Schlitz beer would cause biliousness, as common beer does.

Ask for beer, and you get the beer that best suits your dealer. He may care more for his profit than your health.

Ask for Schlitz, and you get the best beer that the world ever knew.

Ask for the brewery bottling.

J. L. STACK

Notice how Hopkins supported his claims with specific facts and didn't assume prospects knew information his client believed was common knowledge. Too often, we're so close to our companies that it's difficult to realize what prospects truly understand.

Also, Hopkins was a master at educating his readers. When you walk away from reading one of his ads, you feel a little wiser.

And, finally, Hopkins wasn't hesitant about using long copy. He understood prospects crave as much information as possible before making a purchase. After all, who would ever handicap a salesman by only allowing him to speak a certain number of words?

Chapter #26

A Simple Trick to a Memorable Marketing Message

While eating at a Vienna restaurant in the late 1920s, Russian psychologist Bluma Zeigarnik discovered a powerful mental trait you can use to make your marketing message more memorable.

Zeigarnik watched as waiters repeatedly remembered long lists of items ordered by their customers. Once the meals were served, however, the waiters' memories of the items in each order vanished almost immediately.

They could no longer remember what was delivered just minutes earlier.

Zeigarnik was baffled by the waiters' memory loss and went back to her lab to test a theory.

She gave 138 children a series of puzzles and math problems. Shortly after the group started working, she interrupted half the participants mid-task and allowed the other half to complete their assignments.

Just an hour later, only 12% of the children recalled the completed tasks. Conversely, 80% remembered the interrupted tasks.

Repeated experiments confirmed individuals of all ages re-member at least twice as many uncompleted tasks as completed ones.

So how can you apply Zeigarnik's findings to your marketing message so it becomes more memorable?

Begin by using copy that creates curiosity so you develop a level of discomfort in your prospect's mind. In effect, you open a mental loop that can only be closed by a solution you provide.

This tactic is often used in popular television programs such as *Lost*, *Grey's Anatomy*, and *Desperate Housewives*. You're left hanging on an emotional highpoint at the end of an episode. That way you watch the following week to resolve the mystery in your mind.

Below are some bullets I recently wrote to encourage readership of a workers' compensation guide. You'll notice I initiate mental conflict by hinting at solutions. Of course, the complete answers are only revealed to prospects who request and read the guide.

When you read your special report, you'll see how common mistakes can lead an insurance carrier to deprive you of your benefits. You'll also discover ...

- ***An overlooked method for saving your claim if your initial injury notice gets ignored or, worse yet, your boss lies to cover up your request for medical treatment.*** *Be prepared, proof of an injury as provided by co-workers, family or friends does nothing to help you in this situation.*

- ***Why your own doctor's medical advice can jeopardize your claim and prevent you from getting compensation for your current and any future injuries.*** *Make this frequent oversight and your wallet will likely feel as much pain as you.*

- ***The easiest way to ensure an insurance carrier approves medical care for an on-the-job injury, as well as treatment for any previous accidents.*** *Yes, you can even get treatment for nagging injuries that have caused you pain and suffering for years.*

- ***How to determine how much compensation you're entitled to while you recuperate — and what to do if you don't get paid the proper amount.*** *In some situations, you can file multiple claims to get greater compensation.*

Keep in mind, copy that uses the Zeigarnik effect works best when you use it in front of people who are motivated to solve a problem or achieve a goal.

Chapter #27

A Mind-Manipulating Word That Can Create Buyers

I'm about to give you a four-letter word that could make prospects more likely to buy your product or service.

The word's effectiveness is backed by research. But I must admit, until recently, I never saw reference to its use as a mind-manipulating tool in marketing.

This "trick" is detailed in Martin Lindstrom's book, *Brandwashed: Tricks Companies Use to Manipulate Our Minds and Persuade Us to Buy* (great title, isn't it?). In Chapter 6, Lindstrom, a marketing and branding expert who advises top executives at Fortune 100 companies, discusses the role nostalgia plays in marketing. He emphasizes we tend to live in the past — and this is the way our brains naturally function.

As a result, most of us long for things we missed out on in life. We also have preferences for movies, music, trends and products we enjoyed from childhood through our early 20s.

For proof, think about the music you listen to today. Is it the same as what you played on your radio during your teenage and early adult years?

Probably.

Lindstrom says clever companies know our longings for the past become more intense as we get older. So they resurrect the sounds, sights and feelings of their target market's earlier years. They also make reference to the "tricky" word I mentioned above — "time."

Here's an excerpt from *Brandwashed*:

Did you know that just mentioning time in an advertising campaign makes us more likely to buy a product? It's because as soon as we're reminded of how fleeting time is, we think, *I'd better have and enjoy this before it's too late.* And did you also know that when we're "primed" to think about time, the chances we'll feel a personal connection to a product increases exponentially?

For example, if a suitcase manufacturer or coffee company announces, "It's time for a new set of rolling wheels," or "It's espresso time," we're more likely to respond positively to these ads than not. Why? Because time, quite simply, is one thing we all wish we had more of yet rarely give ourselves permission to savor.

So isn't it time you start incorporating this tricky word into your marketing?

Chapter #28

The Headline Genie Who Grants Prospects' Wishes

With proper preparation, the following copywriting tip won't take you long to learn or incorporate into your next marketing piece.

What follows is the easiest strategy for writing powerful headlines that capture attention and keep prospects reading your marketing materials.

But first we must lay some groundwork by identifying your target audience. So who is your market? What are their ages and gender? What is their income level?

Also, what are their biggest concerns, emotions and needs? And what information or help do they need to deal with them?

Once you understand the answers to these questions, you're ready to perform some genie magic. So begin by envisioning yourself having a face-to-face conversation with your ideal prospect.

Now, just like the genie who appears from Aladdin's lamp, imagine telling that prospect you can grant any wish related to your business.

Here's what you might say:

"If I could use my product or service to grant you one wish, what would it be?"

Your prospect's response is what is sometimes labeled a "hidden benefit."

Ted Nicholas, a legendary copywriter, recently revealed he used this same strategy to sell more than 200,000 copies of his book, *How to Form Your Own Corporation Without a Lawyer for Under $75.* His headline read …

The Ultimate Tax Shelter

I recently used this technique to come up with a headline for an IT staffing services company …

Get the Guaranteed Best IT Professionals Whenever You Need Them

Easy stuff, right?

Once you have your "hidden benefit," make sure it's the first copy your prospects see when reading your marketing materials.

Chapter #29

How Much Copy Do You Need to Create a Sale?

T he controversy surrounding long copy vs. short copy is one that won't get settled anytime soon.

After all, it's impossible to determine the exact number of words you need to create a sale because the buying cycle is different for each person.

In some situations, however, you can assume with relative certainty that less information is necessary. For example, prospects shopping on e-commerce websites (e.g., Amazon.com, Zappos.com, Dell.com, etc.) often know what they want and are familiar with the products offered.

As a result, they frequently shop by price. (Usually, more copy is needed for higher-priced items.)

But what if your prospects don't really know you or your company? Worse yet, what if they view your product or service as being just like your competition's?

In these situations, you must educate your target audience — and this approach requires more copy.

Now, before you conclude no one reads long copy, think back to the last time you were passionate about solving a problem. You couldn't consume enough information … you wanted answers to your questions … you craved solutions.

Right?

Well, when you're the one delivering valuable information, you become an authority and a trusted resource. Here are three ways to put yourself in this enviable position:

1. **Get your prospects involved in your marketing message.** Present self-tests, offer free tools and post videos with insight that keeps people coming back to you.

2. **Promote the benefits of your product or service.** Remember, facts about your product or service are features, while benefits explain how those facts positively affect your prospects.

3. **Provide proof elements.** Use testimonials and case studies that explain how you've already helped solve the same problems your clients previously shared with your prospects.

Chapter #30

7 Ways to Get More Responses From Your Marketing Materials

Even if you create copy so compelling it grabs eyeballs like glue, you won't likely get responses unless you include an often-over-looked piece in the persuasion process ...

The call to action.

Far too many opportunities get missed on marketing materials because prospects don't know what step to take next.

If you want your prospects to do something, then you must give them direction. And asking for a sale isn't your only option.

You can also tell prospects to ...

- Download your free report
- Sign up for your e-mail list
- Contact you with questions or information about their situations
- Subscribe to your newsletter or blog feed
- Watch your video tutorial
- Share your material with others
- Visit your profile on social media sites
- Comment on your blog

Here are 7 ways to help you get the responses you want from your marketing materials:

1. **Identify the problem.** The content leading to your call to action should explain and, in many cases, agitate the problem facing your prospects. That way the next step is seen as welcomed solution.

2. **Construct a compelling offer.** You must know what your prospects want and then be willing to give them something that meets their desire.

3. **Start your statement with an action verb.** Express your request with confidence, while avoiding introductory fluff phrases such as "If you are interested," "If we can help," or "If you want to learn more."

4. **Explain the benefits of responding.** Your prospects are skeptical. So tell them what they'll get (and experience) by taking you up on your offer.

5. **Present a single step.** When you overwhelm your prospects with choices, confusion can cause them to do nothing at all.

6. **Contrast with color and avoid clutter.** Clear the space around your call to action and place it in a position your prospects can't miss. On websites, your best bet for immediate attention is "above the fold" (i.e., the portion of a page that displays before scrolling).

7. **Make your request reasonable.** Your opportunity for action declines as you put more obstacles in front of your prospects. So if you require them to provide personal details, don't ask for unnecessary information.

In lengthy marketing pieces, repeat your call to action is several spots. (Websites should have a call to action on every page.)

Also, don't worry if a prospect's initial action isn't a major step in your selling cycle or one that generates revenue. As prospects respond to your marketing materials, their loyalty to you grows and they're likely to make larger commitments later.

Chapter #31

5 Ways to Catch Attention in a Sea of Chaos

When it comes to marketing your business, two variables constantly work against each other.

First, your prospects are inundated with information. From an advertising perspective, the average person is exposed to more than 3,000 messages a day — and most are missed because our society has become so immune to information.

Think about the last time you watched TV, surfed the Web, listened to the radio or talked on the phone. Were you also doing something else at the time?

Maybe the TV was on while you scanned the paper ... maybe you browsed websites during a conference call ... maybe you listened to the radio while talking on your cell phone and driving your car ...

As you can imagine, this multitasking contributes to even shorter attention spans.

The second variable is unfortunate for you and your business — you're starving for attention. But the more messages you put in front of your prospects, the more you contribute to their information overload.

With everyone's brains so stimulated, how can your message cut through the chaos?

Here are five ways:

1. **Focus on "you."** Ever met someone who only talked about himself, laughed at his own jokes and never let you utter a single word? Most company's marketing materials are just like this person because the communication is focused on what they want to say and not what prospects want to read/hear. The words "you" and "how to" tell prospects information is for them.

2. **Deliver on the spot.** You can't let your prospects wait, so give them what they want now. Better yet, provide them with instant value. When you give prospects immediate access to beneficial information focused on them, you get rewarded with action.

3. **Engage the senses.** Remember, the mind "thinks" in images, not words. So use your words to paint a picture of your product or service in action and the end result it offers to your prospects. Work in fears, agitate pains and then promise a better life in some way. And don't hesitate to tell a story.

4. **Provide exclusivity.** Who doesn't like being part of a select group? While everyone else trumpets "me too" promises, your limited-time offer, special privileges or members-only invitations offer your prospects access to something others can only wish they had.

5. **Engage and encourage interaction.** Prospect involvement helps you establish closer relationships and proves you want to better understand your potential customers' needs and desires. As a result, you gain greater trust and, ultimately, more sales.

Chapter #32

12 Methods Guaranteed to Get Your Marketing Message in Front of More Prospects

F ed up with search engine optimization, list buying, networking, advertising and other traditional ways to get your marketing message in front of new prospects?
Here are 12 alternatives you can begin using today:

1. **Send your content as an e-mail.** Your lists of prospects and current customers are the most valuable component in any marketing campaign, so make sure these people are the first to get your new content. Also, encourage interaction by asking for comments and questions.

2. **Post your content on your blog.** The bad news is you're missing considerable traffic and lead-generation opportunities if you don't have a blog. The good news is WordPress (http://www.wordpress.org) makes it easy to get your blog online today.

3. **Distribute your content to article directories.** Three of my favorites are EzineArticles (http://www.ezinearticles.com), Articlesbase (http://www.articlesbase.com) and iSnare (http://www.isnare.com). When you distribute your content, be sure to include a resource box with a call to action that drives people to your website or blog.

4. **Submit your content to bookmarking sites.** OnlyWire (http://www.onlywire.com) allows you to syndicate your blog posts to more than 50 social networking sites, including Digg, Stumbleupon and Reddit, for free with a single click.

5. **Post your content on your Facebook page.** If your Facebook "friends" aren't prospects for your product or service, consider setting up a Facebook page for your business.

6. **Post your content on your Twitter feed.** While you're on Twitter, get involved with conversations. You can also find prospects by searching terms related to problems within your industry using http://www.search.twitter.com.

7. **Post your content to LinkedIn Groups.** Go to http://www.linkedin.com/groupsDirectory and search/register for groups that include your target prospects. Then join the conversations and post links to your content in the Discussions section.

8. **Record your content as a video and distribute it.** Use your content as a script for a video, then upload your file to YouTube or distribute it to several video sharing platforms at once using TubeMogul (http://www.tubemogul.com).

9. **Add your content to an autoresponder.** This step ensures any prospects who sign up for your lists after you distribute your content won't miss your newest tips. What's more, an autoresponder allows you maintain contact with subscribers and share your marketing messages with minimal effort. (The autoresponder service I use is available at http://www.19dollarleadmachine.com.)

10. **Promote your content by commenting on blogs in your industry.** Use http://blogsearch.google.com to find industry-specific blogs and then share insight that encourages people to view additional information on your website and blog.

11. **Post your content as a guest in blogs, newsletters and newspapers.** Contact editors and let them know you have content available that can help their audiences (you may want to write a press release — see Chapter 37). While you're at it, let them know you're available as a source for future articles.

12. **Encourage others to share your content.** Your readers will pass along your content to others — all you have to do is remind them.

The added bonus to the majority of these methods is they won't cost you a single cent to start using right now.

Part IV: **Using Specific Marketing Mediums**

Chapter #33

How to Cut Marketing's Most Costly Expense

Only one factor determines how active a company is with its marketing efforts.

Budget.

There's no way around it. If a business owner or the person responsible for managing the budget doesn't believe there's money for marketing or that the expense won't result in a positive return, then nothing gets done.

Of course, budget is a valid concern. But I'd argue it's given way too much attention because many marketing strategies require minimal investment.

Marketing's most costly expense is the effort put toward getting in front of new targeted prospects.

You might run advertisements ... buy prospect lists ... join organizations or networking groups ... pay for placements in directories ... hold an event ... hire a telemarketing firm ...

Not only do these activities require capital, but you're never guaranteed to get in front of anyone willing to take action on your offer.

One way around this problem is to bring targeted prospects to you, instead of chasing after them. Quite simply, this action of attraction is done by building your own list.

Although list development might seem like a monumental task, I can assure you it's easier than you think — and the rewards are well worth your effort. When you have your own prospect list, you can use e-mail to test new ideas, promote products or services, and drive traffic to your website whenever you want.

After all, how much does it cost you to send an e-mail?

I've stressed the starting point for list building in previous chapters and it's worth mentioning again. Add a lead-capture form to the home page of your website (or, better yet, a squeeze page) and offer information that addresses your prospects' problems in exchange for an e-mail address.

Then, focus your attention on distributing more information that gets prospects in front of your free offer. Begin by making sure your website is optimized well for search engines. This is one of the easiest ways to grow your list without any effort because you naturally attract traffic.

Once that task is complete, create more content related to the information you're giving away. Add the material as new pages on your website and distribute it online and offline. You can also create a blog, record videos, send out press releases, start a newsletter or get articles printed in industry publications.

When your content is used away from your website, include a call to action that drives prospects back to the offer on your home page. Here's a line you often see at the end my articles:

*Get Tom's FREE 21-page guide, **Marketing Materials Made Easy: 8 Secrets for Attracting Attention, Creating Customers and Building Your Business** at http://www. marketingmaterialsmadeeasy.com.*

Chapter #34

Why Even Smart Business Owners (Unknowingly) Market to Blind Eyes

It's astonishing how many smart business owners become victims of a marketing misconception that steals your time and squanders your money.

The problem has to do with numbers.

More specifically, equating successful marketing with the number of people who see your message.

Let me explain …

First, understand there's a difference between marketing to people and marketing to prospects. People become prospects when they take action that demonstrates interest in your product or service (or something similar).

Problems arise when you direct too many marketing resources toward people.

What amplifies the issue are representatives who flaunt advertising and marketing opportunities (e.g., newspapers, radio, TV, Yellow Pages, outdoor displays, etc.) using the number of people the mediums reach. The lure of a large audience then becomes too strong for many business owners to resist.

Now, don't get me wrong.

Sometimes marketing to people is necessary so you can qualify a select few as prospects. But realize there's zero value in marketing to people who see your message and don't take any action.

In effect, these people are blind to anything you put in front of them. Regardless of what you write, say or display, you'll never convince them to act on your offer. So don't blow your budget on people.

On the flip side, prospects — because they expressed interest in what you offer — often become buyers. Therefore, they merit the focus of your marketing efforts (as do your previous clients/customers).

Websites are an especially common place for confusion. Some business owners are fanatical about hits, or the number of times visitors view pages on your website. They assume if hits are high, the website is successful.

A better success indicator is the percentage of visitors who took action and became prospects (i.e., the visitors signed up for an educational guide, requested your newsletter, submitted a question, called your office, etc.).

When your website converts well, hits become a small factor in your website's success.

This quality over quantity principle carries over to other marketing mediums as well. For example, I recently ran a small direct-mail campaign responsible for a boost in my own business. The list was so small most business owners would brush it off as a waste of time.

The campaign only targeted 86 contacts.

My point is this: Most marketing doesn't work because it targets broad audiences of people who will never buy. You're better off using your marketing to qualify your prospects, follow up with consistent communication to establish credibility and trust, and then go after a sale.

Chapter #35

Are You Creating Marketing Assets or Expenses?

One Saturday night, I was on the receiving end of a marketing tactic that I couldn't help but applaud.

My good friend Phil — who I hadn't seen in several months — and I decided to catch up while bar hopping around downtown Phoenix. Our final stop was at a restaurant and wine bar called *Portland's*.

As we sat at the bar, I couldn't help but glance at the menu. I had dinner a couple hours earlier, so I wasn't too hungry.

But the lure of a Sicilian-style sausage and roasted poblano pepper pizza proved too tempting to pass up.

My decision to place an order was rewarded the instant I took the first bite — the pizza was outstanding. So good, in fact, I mentally started planning my next trip to *Portland's*.

But the marketing gods beat me to the punch …

They must have sensed my excitement because, when I received the check, there was a place to include my e-mail address so I could get future discounts and updates.

Whoa … imagine that!

I'm amazed at how few restaurants (and businesses in general) use this marketing tactic. Now *Portland's* has an inexpensive way to stay in contact and encourage me to spend money with them.

Think about it ...

Their list is a marketing asset — the value increases as names get added. Of course, this assumes people on the list receive frequent communication and beneficial information.

You won't find a more valuable marketing asset than your database of contact information for prospects and current/previous customers.

Since these people know you, they're most likely to buy or refer your product or service. So wouldn't you agree growing (and, of course, communicating with) your database should be a priority in your marketing efforts?

This is one reason why I often stress the importance of offering valuable information on your website in exchange for e-mail addresses.

And speaking of marketing assets ...

Every marketing piece you use should generate more in return than what it cost to produce and distribute. So if you have a website ... sales letter ... e-mail campaign ... brochure ... mailer ... whatever ... and it does **not** bring you prospects and generate sales, then re-examine its use.

Can you improve the marketing message? Are you putting the piece in front of the wrong audience? Could you make a stronger offer?

The bottom line is you should make money with your marketing — not just spend it.

Chapter #36

The Dangers of Deciding on a Marketing Budget

Perform a Google search on "how to determine a marketing budget" and you'll get roughly 3.75 million results.

Advice includes everything from using a percentage of revenue and copying your competition to establishing a flat dollar amount and estimating expenditures using past costs.

Of course, these strategies can work. But, in many instances, establishing a firm marketing budget is risky.

Let me explain ...

The reality is marketing budgets are often set at the beginning of the year — before any money is spent. And this creates a problem because there's no way of knowing how much you should allocate if you don't yet know what's working.

Last chapter, I explained the importance of viewing your marketing as an asset, instead of an expense. Truth be told, the reason most business owners establish marketing budgets is because they expect their promotional efforts to fail.

They don't want to lose too much money — and that's understandable.

But if your marketing works and it consistently brings in new prospects, why would you put a limit on how much you spend?

You wouldn't, right?

That would be like avoiding an ATM machine because every time you withdrew $20, your bank deposited $25 into your account.

Now I'm not saying you should spend for the sake of spending. I just want you to reconsider your marketing approach.

Begin by putting tools in place so you can monitor the results of every marketing medium (e.g., e-mail, direct mail, newspaper ads, etc.) you use. If a particular medium isn't working, adjust your copy or stop using it altogether.

(NOTE: Many failed marketing pieces have ego-driven messages that include more oversized logos and company references than helpful information for prospects.)

Keep in mind, if you fail using a particular medium the first time ... or the second ... or even the third, don't automatically assume it doesn't work. Instead, test new variables in front of smaller, targeted audiences.

You see, marketing is a lot like baseball — failure is part of the game. When I played Little League, my dad always reminded me how the best batters at the major-league level fail at least 7 out of 10 times. These days, players who have .300 averages make millions.

Just like the major leaguers, you must continue stepping up to the plate and swinging. You'll eventually connect for a few hits and even an occasional home run.

Chapter #37

How to Incorporate Press Releases Into Your Marketing Strategy

The press release has progressed …

When I entered the newswire business in early 1999, press releases were primarily used by big corporations (especially public companies) to announce major events to journalists.

These days, press releases are no longer just a way to reach media in hopes of getting featured in an article or news story. The audience is much larger now and, thanks to distribution options on the Internet, includes direct access to your buyers.

So what's this mean for you?

Well, first and foremost, you can't limit yourself to only sending press releases for major news announcements. Instead, view your press releases as another vehicle for driving your marketing message to prospects.

With a quick mouse click, you can distribute your press releases to the same circuits, including thousands of online news services and websites, as the corporate giants. Here are a few options to help you get started:

- BusinessWire: http://www.businesswire.com
- PRNewswire: http://www.prnewswire.com
- PRWeb: http://www.prweb.com

As for free options, I find PRLog (http://www.prlog.org) helpful.
When you write your press releases, forget about what you want. Instead, focus on how you can inform or entertain the media's audience. If possible, tie in your topic to a current event.

Also, put yourself in a reporter or producer's shoes. Their audiences demand unique, fresh and relevant information every day. And unless you're Apple, Ford, Microsoft, Amazon.com or a similar corporate heavyweight, the media has little need for a pitch about your new product, website or client.

Not long ago, I sent out a press release that resulted in a 950-word feature in a business publication. The primary content did not include a single word describing my services. Instead, I focused on a topic (how to use marketing to build relationships with prospects and clients) I knew the publication's audience of business owners and executives would find helpful.

Shelf life is another benefit of posting your press releases online. Your news can stick around the Internet for years. So if you optimize your content well with keywords and incorporate links back to your website, your press releases can generate traffic for a long time.

Recently, an editor contacted me because he had space to fill and needed an article fast. After we determined a topic, I scoured the Internet for a source. The person I contacted for my article was listed on a press release that originally ran seven months ago.

So, if you haven't already, begin developing relationships with media members. Pay attention to the writers, reporters, editors and producers who cover topics relevant to your industry. Your effort will improve your chances of becoming a source and help you generate ideas for press release topics.

Chapter #38

Boost Your Marketing Message With This 15-Point Website Content Checklist

Your website content is an essential piece in the persuasion process.

Its effectiveness determines how well your marketing message appeals to your prospects' emotional senses, thus triggering action. The writing on your website also affects whether people can find you and your business using search engines.

When you have poor website content, your ability to collect leads diminishes and your online sales suffer.

I encourage you to save this checklist and set aside a few minutes to review the questions below. Then mark the items that apply to your current website content.

If you're missing more than two of the following 15 items (and please be honest with yourself), then don't wait to adjust your writing.

Are you ready? Here we go ...

1. **Do you have compelling headlines?** Use the text at the top of your content to instantly grab your prospects' attention and encourage further reading.

2. **Have you stated your prospects' problem and explained the need for a solution?** Identify the problem, clarify the need for a fix and then work your product or service into the solution.

3. **Are your words easy to understand?** Write your website content as if it's a one-on-one conversation ("talk" directly to a single prospect), avoid using unfamiliar industry jargon, and match the language your prospects use to describe their situation.

4. **Are keywords incorporated into your content?** Include keywords used by your target audience — and variations of those keywords — in title tags, headers, anchor text and your body content so search engines know what your website is about.

5. **Have you focused on your prospects' needs?** Curb your desire for an instant sale or inquiry and instead offer information that helps address your prospects' problems.

6. **Have you expanded your features to create benefits?** A feature is a fact (e.g., the lawnmower has a 21-inch cutting blade), while a benefit explains an outcome resulting from the feature (e.g., you slice a wider cutting path so you slash your mowing time by as much as 51%).

7. **Have you answered WIIFM?** Explain how your solution addresses the subconscious question your prospects can't ignore — *What's in it for me?*

8. **Do you offer several ways to interact with your prospects?** Encourage involvement by asking for questions or driving prospects to other contact channels (e.g., your Facebook page, Twitter feed, blog, etc.)

9. **Do you have a way to collect your prospects' e-mail addresses?** Allow prospects to qualify themselves and gain knowledge, while you grow a valuable list of people who express a need for your product or service.

10. **Have you linked your content (i.e., anchor text) to other sections of your website?** Direct prospects to internal pages with more in-depth information so they gain a greater understanding of their problem and you keep them on your website longer.

11. **Are your claims backed up with proof?** Incorporate testimonials, case studies, letters of recommendation, media references, published articles, celebrity endorsements and demonstrations of your product or service.

12. **Do you have a call to action?** Tell prospects on every page the specific step you want them to take next.

13. **Is your content "skimmable" with subheads and bullets?** Format your text so it matches the natural reading style of Internet users, which is to skim first and then re-read in more detail.

14. **Is your content free of typos and spelling errors?** Let someone else look over your content so it gets a fresh perspective.

15. **Have you eliminated unnecessary text?** Cut excessive words so you have tighter sentences and clearer ideas.

Chapter #39

The Secret to Solving Your Website Frustrations

When I put my company's first website online in 2001, the Internet was a much different place.

There was far less competition ... Google had yet to establish search engine dominance ... and having a website — much less an online marketing strategy — was far from a necessity.

These days, you likely understand the potential for boosting business online. But, if you're like many business owners, you're still confused on how to properly use your website.

Of course, you know having a website in today's business environment is a must. The problem is it usually requires a significant investment and how you quantify your return isn't always clear.

Right?

Furthermore, if you don't know how to update or make quick changes to your website, it's likely your content sits stagnant and acts as a glorified business card.

So why do some websites bring in business, while others do virtually nothing?

Well, first you must understand the Internet is a marketing medium. And, like other channels such as newspapers, direct mail and TV, successfully capturing leads from your website requires a strategy.

Simply put, a website is not a "build-it-and-they-will-come" marketing medium.

Once you have a strategy in place, the good news is you can leverage technology to automate much of the lead-capturing process. You can also tie in offline marketing with your website and eventually promote offers at virtually no cost.

The secret to solving your frustrations is to view your website as a marketing system — not just a place to post content about your company.

As such, you need …

- Multiple ways to capture e-mail addresses and deliver relationship-building information that addresses your prospects' problems. (Here's one way I handle this task: http://www.squeezepagetutorial.com — you can even try it risk-free or 60 days.)

- The ability to change and add content whenever you want so you don't have to spend time and money every time you create new campaigns. (WordPress eliminates this challenge.)

- Several web forms tied into autoresponders so you can deliver instant information to your prospects when they crave it most.

- A list management software tied into your website so you send targeted e-mails according to your prospects' actions.

- Multiple websites (as well as squeeze or landing pages) so you expand your marketing message, and your online success isn't dependent on a single point of contact.

Once these pieces are in place, you can then track activity and follow up accordingly to turn your prospects into paying clients and customers.

Chapter #40

5 Steps to an Appealing Opt-In Offer

An appealing opt-in offer — or what you give away to prospects in exchange for some piece of contact information — is essential in seeing a return on many marketing investments, especially your website.

Without one, you lose easy opportunities to collect, qualify and communicate with an ever-growing audience that wants to receive your marketing messages. Furthermore, you leave yourself in a dangerous and expensive position because you must always chase leads.

Understand, however, getting anyone to share personal information grows more difficult by the day. So you need an irresistible incentive your prospects can't ignore.

Here's how to create one:

- **Step 1: Brainstorm your prospects' most pressing problems.** Why are they searching for solutions?

- **Step 2: Determine your prospects' desire outcome.** How would their situations be different if the problem you can help solve wasn't part of their lives?

- **Step 3: Decide what you can offer to help prospects achieve their desired outcome.** Do you want to share tips, strategies, methods, formulas, insider advice or something else?

- **Step 4: Figure out the amount you want to give away.** How much information is needed to provide value and still leave ample opportunity for follow-up?

- **Step 5: Explain what your prospects can expect after using your information.** If your prospects take your recommended action, how will their situations change?

E-mail addresses are the most common contact requests on opt-in offers.

For example, on business websites, you often see requests such as "Sign up for our newsletter" or "Sign up for updates." Vague opt-in offers like these might have worked a decade ago, but nowadays you need a stronger appeal. If you offer a newsletter or updates on your website, include several benefits for joining your list.

Or, better yet, come up with a more compelling incentive …

If you're a mortgage broker, you might offer *Insider Secrets to Protecting Your Finances and Getting a Low-Interest Mortgage — Even if You Have Bad Credit.*

If you're a chiropractor, you might offer *3 Easy Exercises That Reduce Lower Back Pain in Just 10 Minutes a Day.*

If you're an estate planning attorney, you might offer *How to Protect Your Assets and Plan Your Estate During Economic Chaos.*

Get the idea?

The bottom line is you must deliver instant value and give prospects a reason to look forward to your future e-mails. If you maintain contact and consistently deliver helpful information, your opt-in list of subscribers will become your most valuable marketing asset.

Chapter #41

How to Win Google's Algorithmic Change Game

When Google announced a major algorithmic adjustment in February 2011, it was expected to have a significant impact on visitors to many websites.

According to Google, the change impacted 11.8% of the search engine's queries and was designed to help its users find more high-quality websites.

Here's an excerpt from the announcement:

> *This update is designed to reduce rankings for low-quality sites — sites which are low-value add for users, copy content from other websites or sites that are just not very useful. At the same time, it will provide better rankings for high-quality sites — sites with original content and information such as research, in-depth reports, thoughtful analysis and so on.*

(You can view the entire announcement here: http://googleblog. blogspot.com/2011/02/finding-more-high-quality-sites-in.html.)

Google has always remained tight-lipped about its ranking algorithms. But one factor is clear — you can get rewarded with traffic (due to higher search engine rankings) if your website delivers information your visitors view as valuable.

Now, I'm a copywriter, not a search engine optimization expert. But, just like you, I understand what type of content is helpful when visiting a website. And it's not the self-serving corporate "speak" you often see with lots of buzz words, company background and mission statements.

Instead, helpful content offers information that addresses the reason you and your prospects visit websites.

Keep in mind, there are only two reasons people use the Internet — they either want entertainment or they need help solving a problem. All other motives fall into one of these two categories.

If you have a business website, then solving a problem is likely the reason your prospects search for you online. So, in order to have a high-quality website in Google's eyes, you need original content, including articles and reports that share insight into your prospects' problems.

Make sense?

When I write website content for clients, I'm often asked about specific topics you should cover in your content. Of course, there are essentials I recommend for websites in all industries (these go beyond your typical home, services, about us and contact pages).

But you also can't go wrong with focusing on a single item …

Value.

Now the bar has officially been raised on what constitutes effective website content. Here are three ways to make sure your website doesn't suffer:

1. **Create quality content.** The message from Google is clear — you need unique content and plenty of it if you expect to attract search engine traffic. Shortcuts such as posting shared content, duplicate reports and automated news feeds now put your website at risk of falling into the depths of search engine abyss. So make a commitment to update your website on a weekly basis.

2. **Nurture your relationships with prospects and clients.** Use your website to interact with your prospects and clients, as well as grow your subscriber list. Remember, the more people know you, the more they're likely to trust you. What's more, when you're in frequent contact with the subscribers on your list, you can drive those people to your website whenever you want.

3. **Deliver your content in a variety of ways.** Video, audio, social networks and press releases are all avenues for expanding the reach of your marketing message and driving traffic to your website. Just like on your website, don't skimp on content quality and present information your prospects view as valuable.

Chapter #42

Is E-mail Marketing Dead?

I f you knew there was an activity nearly all Internet users participate in when visiting websites, you'd be smart to offer that opportunity on *your* website, right?

According recent research released by eMarketer, a digital research and trend analysis company, this recurring activity is subscribing to e-mail lists.

More specifically, the data — compiled from ExactTarget's report, *Subscribers, Fans and Followers: The Social Break-Up* — shows 93% of U.S. Internet users subscribe to permission-based e-mail and get at least one e-mail a day as a result of their subscription activities.

When you combine this detail with ExactTarget's statement that 95% of U.S. online consumers use e-mail, you can understand why e-mail campaigns that complement your website content are so important.

The rapid rise of social media has led some to speculate e-mail is a dying medium. But this claim is far from accurate.

Sure, e-mail is like the old-fashioned grandfather of online marketing, while social media is the sexy supermodel.

But what permission-based e-mail marketing offers is personalized communication to consumers who want to hear from you. And, since e-mail use is so widespread, you know it's a comfortable communication medium for many people.

Furthermore, e-mail delivers an incredibly high return on investment — as much as $43 for every $1 spent (as stated by the Direct Marketing Association).

Here are some quick tips for creating your next e-mail campaign:

- Reward your subscribers by delivering quality content.

- Establish a relationship and build trust before you pitch.

- Trigger involvement by encouraging subscribers to reply back to you with questions.

- Make sure your e-mails are formatted properly for mobile devices.

- Encourage subscribers to share your e-mails with other people.

- Automate some e-mails to save you time and deliver information based on your subscribers' interests.

- Test headlines, copy and offers in your e-mails to improve open rates and click-throughs.

Chapter #43

5 E-mail Marketing Truths You Almost Never Hear

The misinformation circulating among the business community about e-mail's demise as a marketing tool is ridiculous.

Social media killed e-mail … people don't read long e-mails … if you send too much e-mail, people will unsubscribe and label you a spammer … business-related e-mails must use an attention-grabbing template with logos and pictures …

Anyone who consistently markets with e-mail knows these "facts" carry as much truth as a Miss Cleo commercial. The reality is e-mail continues to thrive, even as inboxes get more crowded and the competition for attention increases.

Here are five truths guaranteed to get you more clients using e-mail:

1. **You must send more e-mails to avoid getting labeled a spammer.** Send e-mails only once or twice a month and your unsubscribe rates will soar. After all, people aren't expecting information from you, so they're more likely to view your e-mail as an interruption to their day. Also keep in mind, unsubscribe rates are highest

in the first couple of days after someone subscribes. So immediately send your newest subscribers valuable information.

2. **You must encourage your readers to share your e-mails.** If you provide helpful insight, your e-mails will get passed around. But you should still remind readers to share. So include a sentence in all your e-mails that states something like, "Please feel free to share this e-mail with the people in your network" or "Please feel free to share this e-mail with your friends and family."

3. **You must add more information to your signature line.** You miss a major opportunity for exposure if all you include is your name, phone number or website address in your signature line. Link to an article you wrote, a specific page on your website, a helpful video you recorded, or any other materials that offer valuable information for your readers. One free tool worth checking out is WiseStamp (http://www.wisestamp.com), which links your signature to your social media posts.

4. **You must get people to agree to receive your e-mails.** Don't barge your way into people's inboxes unannounced — you'll get treated as an uninvited guest. Make sure anyone you send to has agreed to receive your e-mails. You can do this by using an e-mail marketing software (such as AWeber, iContact or InfusionSoft) to confirm every opt-in you receive.

5. **You must optimize your e-mails for easy reading on smart phones.** As much as 82 percent of people who have smart phones use their devices for reading e-mails. That's a huge audience that may miss your messages. So check with people in your office to see how your e-mails show up on their devices. If your e-mails don't display properly, you need to change your format.

Chapter #44

The 4 U Checklist for Writing Irresistible E-mail Subject Lines and Headlines

Before you can get your marketing message in front of your prospects' eyeballs, you must first attract their attention. And that's where a headline or, in the case of e-mail, a subject line becomes your best asset.

The following four criteria for writing headlines and e-mail subject lines were developed by Michael Masterson, a renowned giant in the direct-response industry who's sold more than a billion dollars worth of products and services.

So here are the 4 U's ...

1. **Urgent — Almost everyone's natural tendency is to procrastinate.** So give your readers a reason to react now. Try targeting a pressing issue you know your prospects can't stop thinking about or maybe you might make a limited-time offer in your headline or subject line.

2. **Unique — Say something new or, if you have something familiar, say what you're offering in a new way.** Also, avoid clichés and overused phrases that have lost their meaning over time (e.g., "get the _____ everyone is talking about," "we're the solution you've been looking for," "we're here for you," etc.). The bottom line is you need to get creative.

3. **Ultra-Specific — Present stats or figures or even promise an exact outcome.** For example, I have a free training on my website at http://www.writewaysolutions.com called *7 Days to a More Persuasive, Lead-Generating Marketing Message*. The outcome is you'll learn how to create a persuasive marketing message. I'm also specific in telling you it will only take 7 days.

4. **Useful — Provide insight so valuable you actually reward prospects for reading your marketing materials.** Is what you're stating in your headline or subject line so beneficial that it instantly captures your prospects' attention?

In addition to writing headlines and subject lines, the Four U's can also apply to your bullets and subheads. Of course, matching your copy to this checklist requires extra time. But as Masterson's sales history proves, your effort gets rewarded.

Chapter #45

E-mail Marketing: Why List Size is a Small Piece of the Promotional Puzzle

If there's a single stumbling block preventing business owners from doing more e-mail marketing, it's the size of their lists.

Either they don't have one or there's concern because the number of e-mail addresses on their lists are too few to make the effort worthwhile.

So does size *really* matter?

The simple answer is no.

I'll let you in on a little secret. My list isn't large compared to most e-mail marketers. But if you're on my list, you notice this doesn't prevent me from communicating with you on a regular basis.

That's because, when doing e-mail marketing, your list is a small piece of the promotional puzzle. In fact, you ignore major opportunities for expanding your marketing reach when you spend time writing an e-mail and then only send it to your list(s).

Your list size isn't nearly as important as the way you communicate with the people on it. When you focus on delivering value and building relationships, any e-mail you write can be used in several other ways to reach new customers.

Fortunately, these other distribution options take minimal time, money and effort.

- **Post your e-mail to your website.** E-mails are a great way to keep content fresh on your website. In addition, if you're addressing prospect problems, you'll likely attract traffic to your website from people using search engines to find solutions.

- **Post your e-mail to your blog.** Just like your website, you must keep content fresh on your blog. A properly formatted blog will also attract search engine traffic. If you don't have a blog, start one soon. It's one of the easiest ways to position yourself as an industry authority.

- **Post your e-mail as an article on article directories.** You'll almost always get the most traffic using EzineArticles.com, although there are thousands of other article directories online. EzineArticles.com, Articlesbase.com, GoArticles.com and iSnare.com are some of my favorites.

- **Use your e-mail as a script for a video.** Simply present your e-mail as if you're standing in front of an audience. Then, post your video on YouTube.com. (Be sure you use keywords in your file name, title, description and tags.) You can expand your video distribution using a service such as TubeMogul.com.

- **Link to your e-mail using social media.** Once your e-mail is available online, link to it from Facebook, Twitter, LinkedIn and other social networking sites. (The Groups section on LinkedIn is a great place for finding and communicating with prospects.) Do a little searching online and you'll find several tools that automate this task and post to all your social media accounts at the same time.

- **Reformat your e-mail and send it to the media as a press release.** Writers, editors and producers are always looking for qualified sources to interview for story topics. An informative press release that addresses your prospects' problems positions you as an industry authority eager to share knowledge.

- **Combine several e-mails to create a special report.** This is one of the most effective ways to repurpose your e-mails. Your special report will add more prospects to your list when you use it as an incentive on lead-capture pages, advertisements, forum messages, guest blog posts, etc.

Chapter #46

7 Mistakes That Get Your Autoresponder E-mails Trashed

The autoresponder can transform any lifeless website into a lead-generating engine that continuously drives your marketing message in front eager prospects — whether you're sitting at your desk or poolside under a cabana at a Caribbean resort.

After all, once you set up a series of e-mails, you're done.

Sure, you must get traffic to your website or squeeze page so prospects opt-in to your list. But once they become subscribers, you can personalize your marketing message and automate its delivery over a set period of time.

(If you're not familiar with autoresponders and how they work, watch this 5-minute video: http://www.youtube.com/watch?v=9wmChqTeqgo.)

The benefits of using autoresponders seem almost too good to be true, especially considering the minimal investment they require (some services even let you set up free campaigns). Unfortunately, their simplicity leads many to overlook important factors that can result in your e-mails finding a permanent place in the trash bin.

The 7 most common mistakes that cause autoresponder e-mails to get ignored are listed below. When you read through them, notice how several can also apply to your everyday e-mails.

- **Mistake #1: Flubbing the From section.** Don't include anything but a person's name in the From section of your e-mails. Have you ever seen a company, product or publication write and send an e-mail? Of course not ... e-mails are personal because they're written and read by people.

- **Mistake #2: Snubbing your subject line.** Like your From section, a company, product or publication name in your Subject lines does little to get your e-mails opened. Dedicate the same attention to your Subject lines as you give to headlines — create curiosity, deliver news and stress benefits.

- **Mistake #3: Crafting a corporate essay.** Write in simple, easy-to-understand English. Your e-mails are no different than one-on-one conversations, so mimic the way you speak. Provide plenty of breaks in your copy (yes, one-sentence paragraphs are fine), use short words and sentences, and present questions to encourage interaction.

- **Mistake #4: Sending only to sell.** Of course, you'll occasionally have a product or service you want to promote in an e-mail. But first deliver valuable content to prove to your subscribers that what you send them is worth reading. That way they look forward to seeing your name in their inbox.

- **Mistake #5: Muddling your message with graphics.** To many people, an e-mail heavy with graphics is an instant sign of a sales message. What's more, some images and formatting can make your text difficult to read. So keep your autoresponder e-mails as visually simple as the e-mails you send to friends and family.

- **Mistake #6: Overlooking a call to action.** Never assume your subscribers know what to do next. Whether you want them to read another article, visit your Facebook page, send you questions or click a buy button, make sure the next step is clearly stated.

- **Mistake #7: Sending off-topic e-mails.** If your subscribers signed up for bird bath cleaning tips, don't expect them to respond to your latest offer for designer dog sweaters. You'll lose the credibility you built in previous messages the instant an off-topic e-mail hits a subscriber's inbox.

And, finally, when deciding on topics for your next autoresponder series, keep your ears open. What questions do you often hear? What keeps your prospects up at night? What's getting mentioned in the media?

Chapter #47

How to Avoid Creating a Terrible Tagline

L et's play a quick game of tagline trivia ...
Read the following taglines and match each one with the correct business:

1. We want to help you.
2. The lowest prices around.
3. The best quality and service.

a. 1st Choice Bail Bonds
b. Livery Distribution
c. Big Al's

I collected these taglines one morning while driving my son to school. You probably see similar marketing messages in your neighborhood.

The problem most taglines share is they lack meaning. Besides a release from behind bars, do you understand what the above businesses offer?

I don't. In fact, I'd argue the three taglines could apply to just about any company.

Like any weapon in your marketing arsenal, taglines must deliver a beneficial message to your prospects. **If you use a tagline and it doesn't state in a handful of words the solution delivered by your product or service, you're wasting valuable space on your marketing materials.**

Your prospects don't have the time or interest to figure out what you can do for them. They have pressing problems that require immediate solutions.

Sure, you see well-known companies use vague taglines all the time. Coke … McDonalds … Nike … Apple … Chevrolet … Prudential …

But these are deep-pocketed corporations that can repeatedly force-feed you marketing messages until your mind can't resist them anymore. You don't have this financial luxury!

See how your tagline matches up against this checklist:

- **Can your text stand alone?** If you remove your company name and other surrounding words, is your message still effective?

- **Does your text only apply to your business — not your competitors?** Do you have a distinctive message?

- **Is the outcome clear?** Can everyone understand what they get by doing business with you?

- **Does your text avoid worn-out clichés?** Haven't we seen enough tired promises with words such as "quality," "value," "best," "satisfaction," "leading," and "maximize"?

- **Would your words attract you as a prospect?** Does your message focus on your target audience, instead of your business?

Chapter #48

What Feature Does Facebook's Most Successful Businesses Share?

Although I'm pretty active on Facebook, I haven't mentioned it much in previous chapters.

For many businesses, engagement on Facebook has become the cornerstone for social media success. The key, however, is being able to attract attention.

Fortunately, you have an advantage because you're different than your competitors — you have unique characteristics. In some cases, these traits may naturally help you or your business stand out ... and that's a good thing.

After all, there's a strong chance you're targeting the same prospects on Facebook as your competitors.

But here's the problem (and this is critical) ...

The vast majority of Personal and Business Fan Pages on Facebook share the same appearance and have limited functionality.

You've seen the pages, right?

A name across the top, picture in the upper-left corner with contact information below it, ads along the right column, and posts down the center.

There are no variations in colors either. Furthermore, you can't "welcome" visitors ... you can't capture leads ... and you can't add custom graphics (unless you know how to recode your page).

From a marketing perspective, Facebook's Personal and Fan Page templates instantly put you at a deadly disadvantage because you display no differences between you and your competition. You've leveled the playing field, making it impossible to secure space in your prospects' minds.

But a positive differentiation (as discussed in earlier chapters) causes your prospects to perceive you or your product or service as being better. For proof, look no further than the most successful brands on Facebook ...

Coca-Cola ... Pringles ... Honda ... Starbucks ... Walgreens ... Adidas ... Red Bull ...

What's the one quality these companies share?

They all have **custom** Facebook Fan Pages.

The potential for expanding the reach of your marketing message on Facebook is tremendous.

Not only is it the world's fastest-growing social network with more than 500 million users, but more than half of those people login to the service every day. And, as you know, Facebook isn't the type of site where people just hop on for a minute or two every couple of weeks — they participate daily and engage often for hours at a time.

Facebook's tremendous growth can be attributed in large part to one social factor:

Friendcasting.

So what is "friendcasting"?

Basically, this term describes the way users share news, pictures, videos and links with others on the Internet. The popularity of this practice is expanding so fast that some studies show Facebook is now the top source for driving traffic to places such as Yahoo! and MSN (Bing) — even surpassing Google.

So what does this mean for you?

Quite simply, you can deliver your message to a larger audience — and dedicate less time, money and effort doing so.

Let me explain ...

People now spend less time searching on their own. Instead, they explore recommendations from friends or start searches based on others' activities. What's more, people are more eager than ever to share their own information.

As a result, one connection with a "fan" on Facebook can lead to thousands of brand impressions with a single click of your mouse.

Your visibility also multiplies because each post on your Fan Page displays on all your fans' pages as well. So your only job is to provide "shareworthy" experiences and ideas.

Now sure, many individuals and companies now have Facebook Fan Pages because they make growing an online community super easy.

But how much are "fans" of these pages really worth?

According to research conducted by Vitrue, a social media management company, each Facebook fan is worth about $3.60 a year (see the report here: http://vitrue.com/blog/2010/04/14/360-facebook-fan-valuation-is-just-the-tip-of-the-iceberg/).

Of course, that return is greater for some companies because of the social engagement tools on Fan Pages, such as clicks, comments, likes, plays and shares — which can trigger a viral effect.

At first glance, you might think $3.60 seems minimal. However, that number quickly multiplies when you factor in the average number of fans on a typical Facebook Fan Page.

Sysomos, a social media monitoring and analytics firm, puts the estimate at 4,596 fans. Do the math and you'll discover ...

That's an extra $16,545.60 in revenue each year.

Sysomos' research also revealed Facebook fans spend more money. Their study detailed in *The Value of a Facebook Fan: An Empirical Review* estimates that someone who "Likes" a brand will spend an average of $71.84 more each year on that company's products or services than someone who has not Liked it on Facebook.

Crazy, isn't it?

Chapter #49

Why So Many Print Ads Fail

I f you're not getting the leads you want from your print ads and you can't figure out what's going wrong, you can likely trace your problem to one of the three common mistakes mentioned below.

Let's begin by thinking about the way you read a newspaper or magazine. How do you determine what articles get read?

Since there's so much text and you can't read it all at once, you probably scan until a headline grabs your attention.

Right?

Then, once you're hooked by the headline, you read deeper into the article.

Well, your ad is no different — it needs a headline to attract attention. There are no exceptions to this rule.

Pick up today's newspaper or scan your Yellow Pages and I guarantee you'll see very few headlines in the ads. And, keep in mind, a company name or your logo is NOT a headline.

(Your company name and logo offer zero benefits to your prospects, so they have no effect on a purchasing decision. As such, neither one should be a focal point in your ads.)

Your headline's sole purpose is to provide a reason for prospects to continue reading your ad. When you don't have one, you leave little reason to move deeper into your copy. So, first, use your headline to deliver a strong benefit that appeals to your prospects' desires.

Next, you must have an offer. This is where you want to deliver value and reward readers for their time. If your product or service is priced greater than about $20, you're better off not trying to sell it in most ads because you don't have enough space for a persuasive message.

Instead, provide a way to introduce your prospects to your product or service. You can do this by offering free reports, articles, checklists, self-tests, trials, etc. This allows you to build the credibility and trust you need to create a sale.

As part of your offer, make taking action easy and, if possible, allow prospects to get immediate information without human interaction.

For best results, direct your offer to one type of prospect. For example, if you're a lawyer who provides criminal, divorce and bankruptcy legal services, use separate offers and ads for each area of law. The prospects for these three services are different and, as a result, so are the reasons they would act on your offer.

Makes sense, doesn't it?

And, third, tell prospects exactly what you want them to do after reading your ad. This critical step is often referred to as your "call to action." **If you don't explain what to do next, you risk leaving the decision up to your prospects. And, in most cases, they won't do anything.**

Or course, a successful advertisement requires several other components. But these are the three I most often see missed when I do ad critiques.

By the way, unless you have an unlimited marketing budget, using your ads to build brand awareness will only lead to frustration. Leave this tactic up to the heavy-hitters you often see in Super Bowl spots, such as Coke, Pepsi, Budweiser and GoDaddy. They have budgets to burn and can wait for buyers. You don't have that luxury.

Chapter #50

An Easy Way to Increase Your Ad Readership by Up to 700%

When you open a newspaper, magazine or similar publication, which are you more likely to read — the ads or articles?

In most cases, I bet you seek out the articles. Right?

People are drawn to articles because they include newsworthy items or, at the very least, topics that pique interest. In fact, research shows articles and news stories receive anywhere from 500%-700% greater readership than ads.

If you do any advertising, then I encourage you to use the above statistic to your advantage. The easiest way is to write and design your "ads" so they don't look like ads.

You see, the problem with most ads is they're boring. The ads look the same, offer identical information and provide little benefit to readers.

When your ads share characteristics with others in your industry, it's impossible for you to attract attention.

Remember, people read newspapers, magazines and periodicals for news — not information about your company, images of your logo or fancy fonts showing your company name.

So give them news in your ads!

Furthermore, use the same font, style, spacing and layout as the articles in the publications you advertise in. That way readers are less likely to associate your piece with all the other ads.

Of course, changing your ads so they deliver newsworthy information requires longer copy.

In the early 1900s, Maxwell Sackheim wrote the famous *Do You Make These Mistakes in English?* ad to promote an English mail-order course by Sherwin Cody. The ad was so successful it ran for 40 years without any changes.

And guess what?

The ad used long copy and delivered news readers could immediately use. Check it out:

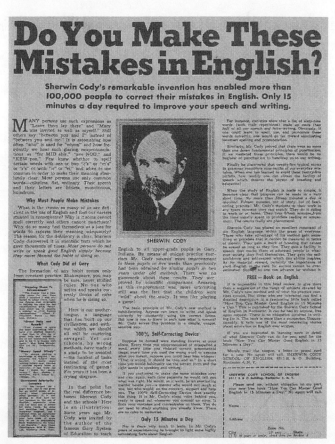

Your prospects see hundreds of ads a day. Make sure yours isn't among the majority they ignore.

Chapter #51

How to "Squeeze" More Leads from Your Online Marketing Efforts

O nce you start marketing online, it doesn't take long to realize generating leads is no easy task.

The competition is fierce because the audience is huge. So attracting attention, establishing your credibility and creating a compelling offer are essential.

The problem you face is most online consumers do not buy the first time they visit a website.

For proof, consider your own buying behavior. The last time you shopped — whether it was online or offline — did you first collect information and compare prices, or did you pull out your wallet at the first opportunity?

When you don't provide prospects with a reason to return to your website, you lose opportunities for sales. This is why building an online prospect list is critical to marketing success on the Internet.

Once prospects register for your list, you can deliver more content that establishes your credibility, while also giving them reasons to collect more information and return to your website.

One quick and easy way to grow your list is through a squeeze page. A squeeze page is essentially a condensed website with one page and a single objective …

Collect e-mail addresses.

When prospects arrive at your squeeze page, they can either enter an e-mail address to receive some type of free information or leave without doing anything — there are no other options.

To see an example, check out http://www.howtopersuadepro-spects.com.

Roughly half the people who visit the above squeeze page submit their e-mail addresses and instantly receive the free video (you may have been one of them). I have several squeeze pages online targeting different areas of direct-response copywriting and marketing. Each one is adding names to my prospect list at all times.

You can do the same thing with your online marketing efforts. Simply come up with incentive — such as an article, report, video, checklist, consultation, subscription or e-course — that helps solve a problem your target prospects share.

Applications such as WordPress make setting up your own squeeze page a snap (you can check out the software I use and try it risk-free for 60 days at http://www.squeezepagetutorial.com).

In addition to the benefits discussed earlier, a squeeze page gives you an immediate advantage over your competition because ...

- **You can instantly qualify your leads and screen out unwanted prospects.**

- You can drive targeted traffic from prospects who use search engines such as Google, Yahoo! and Bing.

- **You can establish yourself as an expert in your area of business and emphasize your competitive advantages.**

- You can set up an automated e-mail marketing campaign to maintain contact with your prospects and customers.

- **You can initiate a channel of communication that allows you to discover your prospects' desires related to your product or service.**

Keep in mind, squeeze pages are not intended as website replacements. Instead, they're designed to complement the information on your website and spread your marketing message to a wider online audience.

For example, let's say you're a personal injury lawyer looking to attract leads from people hurt in accidents. A squeeze page would help you attract prospects for each type of accident — in addition to the leads you already generate from your website.

Depending on the type of prospect you want, you could create separate squeeze pages for accidents with semi trucks, cars, motorcycles, trains, pedestrians, etc. As an incentive to collect your prospects' e-mail addresses, you'd offer a free piece of information specific to each type of prospect.

Make sense?

From a search engine optimization perspective, there are ways to make your squeeze pages more appealing.

First, choose a keyword-rich domain that matches your prospects' search history. So if you want to attract victims of motorcycle accidents in Kirkland, Washington, your URL might be http://www.kirklandmotorcycleaccidentattorney.com.

(By the way, the *exact* keyword combination in the above domain gets 36 searches a month. That might not seem like a huge number. But imagine how many of those inquiries you'd get if you had a squeeze page at the top position in Google.)

Don't make the mistake of going after super competitive keywords with your squeeze pages. You're more likely to get ranked higher and faster with less competitive terms (often containing three or more words). You'll find these "long-tail" keywords often generate more qualified leads from people further along in the sales process.

Of course, the same SEO formatting with keywords on your website also applies to your squeeze pages. So you'll want your keywords in your title tags, headline, headers and body text.

Here are several additional ways to make your squeeze pages more effective:

- **Keep your design simple.** You don't want anything to distract your prospects from registering for your free information (so make sure your call to action is obvious).

- **Have a powerful headline.** Use this text to immediately appeal to your prospects' needs.

- **Use bullets to explain the benefits of your offer.** Remember, facts are features, while benefits explain how those facts positively affect your prospects.

- **Test adding a video.** Some people would rather watch video than read text.

- **Add social proof.** Display comments that prove to your prospects the information you offer was already used successfully by people just like them.

Chapter #52

Why Kindle Should Play a Part in Your Marketing Efforts

The process people use to gather information is always evolving. Case in point ...

According to a study released by the *Association of American Publishers*, e-book sales in February 2011 — for the first time — topped all other formats, including paperbacks and hardcovers.

E-books (and their associated e-readers) have clearly found a place in people's personal libraries. In fact, some publishing experts predict e-book sales will comprise up to 25% of all book sales within the next 2-3 years.

If you use educational materials to market your business, this news should get you excited. After all, making your marketing materials available to an audience who enjoys reading on electronic devices is relatively easy and doesn't require a big budget.

What's beneficial about Kindle is your marketing materials aren't only available to the device's users. They're also accessible on iPads, iPhones, Android phones and many other mobile devices (even your Windows PC).

Furthermore, you can't argue with the instant credibility that comes with being listed as an Amazon.com author. And, if you make your Kindle e-book available for purchase, the monthly checks from Amazon.com are a nice bonus, too.

Now, here's an important fact to remember ...

You only need a special report or collection of articles — not an entire book — to publish on Kindle and get listed on Amazon. com.

In fact, prior to this book, my most recent Kindle e-book was a special report.

A major advantage of the free Kindle Direct Publishing platform at http://kdp.amazon.com is the ease at which you can make changes. You can adjust keywords, modify your description and even alter the text in your "e-book" whenever you want. You can even experiment with different price points.

And, since you don't have to worry about the demands of a publisher, you maintain complete control over your material. So you can even promote your products or services!

Chapter #53

How to Use Your Business Card as a Lead-Generating Marketing Piece

Not long ago, I went to a networking event.

It had been several months since I attended what essentially has become a business card exchange. Now, don't get me wrong, I want my business card in people's hands.

But I'm hesitant to give it to just anyone.

After all, my business card is a marketing piece. So it only belongs in front of targeted prospects.

While at the event, I noticed people peddling business cards like napkins at a fast-food joint. Bundles were tossed on tables ... dropped in bowls ... and used as paper for jotting notes.

The idea that someone would want your business card just because you're in the same room seems bizarre.

Nevertheless, plenty of people vigorously passed out business cards — sometimes without even saying a word to the person on the receiving end. In most cases, the number of passed out business cards seemed to take precedence over the quality of contacts.

If you're willing to think beyond the norm, your business card can offer incredible opportunities as a lead-generating marketing piece. Here are a few ideas:

First, who says you must use a standard 3.5- x 2-inch size for your business card? Marketing is all about standing out and attracting attention. If your business card looks like everyone else's, how can you expect anyone to give it a second look?

I use a fold-over money card to draw interest to my business card (you can view a sample here: http://www.thefoldovermoneycard.com). As you can imagine, recipients do a double-take every time they see it. What's more, they eagerly show my business card to other people (and even request additional business cards to give away).

Second, there's no rule against including more than your name, title, company name and contact phone/e-mail on your business card. The truth is this information is worthless unless your prospect knows one piece of critical marketing information — what your product or service can do for them.

For example, in addition to contact information, my business card has a headline that reads, *"Stop Driving Away Customers and Bleeding Profits from Your Business with Poor Marketing Materials ... TODAY!"* I then go on to explain, *"I'll help you create compelling copy that attracts greater attention, persuades your prospects faster and puts more profit in your pocket."*

And here's one final idea to consider ...

Do you agree you'd benefit by knowing if someone was truly interested in your product or service and not just leaving your business card in the nearest circular file? If so, then use your business card to give people a reason to visit your website. That way you can collect names and e-mail addresses to grow your prospect list.

Here's the exact wording from my business card: *"Grab your FREE tips for increasing responses on your advertisements, websites, brochures, letters, e-mails and more at http://www.writewaysolutions.com/blog."* When someone visits my website, I offer them a free special report in exchange for an e-mail address. As a result, it becomes easy to deliver more value and stay in contact with prospects long after they see my business card.

Chapter #54

14 Common Mistakes That Reduce Readership and Create Falling Response Rates (Audio Transcript)

Tom: Hello, everyone. This is Tom Trush, and today we're discussing critical mistakes that can reduce readership on your marketing materials. I have a list of 14 common mistakes that we will go through.

On the line today, I have my twin brother Dale. If you are familiar with some of the trainings I've done, you'll also be familiar with Dale. He's been on other calls, including the training call on e-mail marketing. Dale, would you like to say a quick hello and give a little background about yourself?

Dale: I'd be happy to, Tom. Hello, everyone. My name is Dale Trush. As Tom mentioned, I'm his twin brother. I have worked 13 years in the communications, broadcasting, public relations, media relations and marketing industries. The last six years, I have worked with a Fortune 500 financial services company here in the Midwest.

I'm looking forward to having this conversation with you, Tom. Fourteen sounds like a great number to cover.

Tom: Excellent, Dale. One of the reasons I have Dale on the call is that there are certain insights Dale can offer that can complement the advice I give. I mostly deal with entrepreneurs and small business owners; whereas, Dale works in the corporate world. Things can be a little bit different at that level than it is at the entrepreneurial or small business level.

Dale: And Tom, in case we also have any listeners or readers who may be working in the nonprofit world, I can offer some perspective from there, as well, because I worked for four years for a national non-profit children's wish granting organization. I think we can cover this from a lot of different perspectives today.

Tom: Excellent. Well, let's get right into it. We'll start off with the first mistake, and this is something I see all the time. It's the first step I take when I am critiquing copy for people. I go through the copy and look for the following words: *we*, *our*, and their *company name*. I want to see how many times the words *we, our,* or a *company name* are included in the copy, and compare those with the number of times the words *you, your* or *you're* are mentioned in the copy. Why do I do this?

Well, you want your copy to be very conversational. You want to imagine your copy is speaking to someone as if it's a one-on-one conversation. You'll often see the words *we, our* or the *company name* either at the beginning of sentences or somewhere else in the copy, but repeated over and over again. Consecutive sentences will often start with the word *we*. Then they'll go to *our* and then they'll go to *we* again. "We can do this and we can do that for our clients."

When you read that, subconsciously, the message comes across as not being addressed to the prospect. Instead, it's all about the company. I use the analogy that it's very similar to being at a party.

Say you meet a guy at a party and all he does is talk about himself or laugh at his own jokes. He'll have a story that tops whatever story anybody else can say. We've all met that type of person before.

When your copy is all about your company and not about your prospects, then you're just like that person at a party. I encourage people, as one of the first steps in critiquing their own copy, to check for these words.

An easy way to do this is to make two columns on a piece of paper. In the left column, note all the times you find the words *we, our,* and then your *company name*. In the right-hand column, note all the times you find *you, your,* and *you're*. Then tally them up.

There isn't an exact percentage that you want to have for the *you's, your's* in comparison to the *we's, our's* and *company names*, but you want to have significantly more instances of *you's* and *your's*.

Imagine yourself talking to somebody in a face-to-face conversation. You're going to use lots of *you's* and *your's*. You want to make that copy comfortable for your prospects when they read that.

I mentioned a study that was done by the psychology department at Yale University in a recent article I wrote. They studied consumers' reactions to certain words in advertisements. The results were compiled to create the 12 most persuasive words to consumers.

You can probably guess that the most persuasive word was *you*. The study did multiple tests, and in every test, *you* was listed as the most persuasive word. The other most persuasive words were *money, save, new, results, health, easy, safety, love, discovery, proven* and *guaranteed*.

These are some other words you want to try working in to your copy. But if you just want to focus on one, then I can't recommend the word *you* enough. Put that in your copy as many times as possible.

I don't know if you have a few thoughts on that, Dale, with the use of *you* in copy in comparison to *we, our* and then *company name*.

Dale: I couldn't agree with you more, Tom. To simply reiterate, the techniques you're describing are going to make the copy much more engaging for the client or potential customer. You're right on target.

Tom: There's one other point I wanteto bring up with the use of *you's* and *your's*, and that's the subconscious issue that your prospects can't ignore. Let's dig a little deeper into this mistake.

When most people write a marketing piece, a lot of times they think *What can I write that will create a sale?* Of course, you want to create a sale and that is the ultimate result, but that's the wrong way to approach a marketing piece. You always have to think about the subconscious question your prospects can't ignore, and that question is *What's in it for me?*

While you go through your copy, comparing the *you's* and *your's* to the *we's, our's* and *company names,* you also want to see how your copy is answering that question — *What's in it for me?* When your prospects read, that's what they're thinking subconsciously: *What's in it for me?*

If they don't get that answer, they will stop reading. You've totally lost them. You'll reduce the readership. You won't even give them an opportunity to respond to your copy.

Dale, when you're writing copy, is that something you think about as well?

Dale: You hit the nail on the head, Tom. I can tell you that whether you're working in the nonprofit sector or you're working in the corporate world, you always make it as clear as possible to the potential customer or client *What's in it for me.* I call it the "WIIFM." That's the acronym for *What's in it for me.*

I can even give you a real-world example. I'm currently rewriting a brochure about different investment programs because the former writer never included the *What's in it for me* angle. Now we have to rewrite everything that left out the "WIIFM."

Tom: I have to imagine since that question is not getting answered in the copy you're rewriting right now, you're probably noticing a lot of *we's*, *our's* and references to the *company name.* Is that true?

Dale: You're exactly right, Tom. As a matter of fact, it does a great job of explaining funds and investment strategies, but it never actually translates it down to the client and tells them what's in it for them, what's in it for the client.

It's like the copy hits a roadblock and then never travels all the way to the client. It's not having the desired effect. Now we have to take the time to rewrite it to include the *What's in it for me* from a client's perspective.

Tom: I imagine there will be significant changes to that piece.

Dale: Absolutely. I've rewritten the entire thing from A to Z. For our listeners, it's going to save you time, money and resources if you simply focus on *What's in it for me* from a customer's perspective. Focus on that from the beginning, and you're already winning a good portion of the battle.

Tom: Let's go onto the second mistake. Mistake #2 is not having a headline. This is something I see repeatedly. Your prospects read your marketing piece like they read a newspaper.

When you read a magazine or newspaper, you scan through to look for something that draws your interest so you can keep on reading. I can't tell you how many times I come across marketing pieces where there's no headline at all, or there's a headline that really does not offer any incentive for a reader to continue going deeper into the copy.

I give many tips on how to write headlines, including formulas that people can use to write headlines. I'll give you a great tip that anyone can use to write a headline. If you're stumped, and you just don't know how to get a prospect's attention with a headline, then I recommend you use the following tip:

Become a headline genie.

Just imagine yourself standing in front of your ideal prospect. You tell your prospect that he or she has a wish, and whatever that wish is, you will be able to grant it. Think about what that prospect's response would be. What would that client want most from your business? Take whatever that response is and turn that into a headline.

By doing this, you figure out what your prospects want. In marketing, you want to enter the conversation that's going on in your prospect's mind. By using this exercise, by imagining yourself as a headline genie granting your prospect's greatest wish, you're stepping into that conversation that your prospect is already having. This is very powerful. It's going to attract their attention and keep them reading.

That is the ultimate goal with the headline. You don't want to think of a headline as being something that's immediately going to generate a sale. That's the wrong way to think about your headline. The headline's job is to get your prospect to continue reading to the first sentence of your piece. The job of your first sentence is to get the prospect to read the second sentence.

Think of your marketing piece as little steps your prospects must take. You want to get the prospect to move from line to line. Don't overwhelm yourself and think *I've got to create a headline that's going to generate this instant sale*. That's the wrong way to approach it. You just have to think about what you can include in your headline to get your prospect to the first sentence.

Any thoughts on that one, Dale?

Dale: Again, you're exactly right. If you look at a big paragraph of text with no headline, that's very oppressive. You're going to say to yourself, *I don't want to read that*. This brochure that I'm rewriting has big, long paragraphs without headlines.

Big blocks of text without headlines are scary to a reader. A reader wants a headline that moves them into the lead sentence and a lead sentence that leads them to the second sentence. Before you know it, you've got them reading the entire thing.

Tom: That's a good point, Dale. Without a headline, you're not even giving your prospect an opportunity to get deeper in, because there's no incentive, and it can be overwhelming to see all the text. That text will never get read.

Quite frankly, you're making it difficult for your prospects to read that marketing piece. You want to get your point across and make it easy to understand. We all want things quick and easy. If your marketing piece isn't portraying that thought, then you're losing out on a lot of opportunity.

One important element of a good headline deals with the subconscious, and that is *curiosity*. We're naturally born with a desire to know more than what we already know. And arousing curiosity can be very effective in your marketing piece.

I want to tell you a story that touches on curiosity from the 1920s. There was this Russian psychologist, Bluma Zeigarnik who discovered a really powerful method that you can use to make your marketing message more memorable.

She was in a restaurant eating, and she watched as waiters would repeatedly remember these long lists of items ordered by their customers. Once the meals were served, the waiters couldn't remember the lists of items. They couldn't remember what they had just delivered only minutes earlier.

Zeigarnik, a psychologist, was baffled by the waiters' memory losses. She decided to conduct a test to see why these waiters couldn't remember orders after they delivered them.

She gave 138 children puzzles and math problems. She let the children start working, but then she interrupted half the participants midtask, while allowing the other half to complete their assignments. An hour later, she found that only 12 percent of the children recalled completed tasks, but then 80 percent of the other group remembered the interrupted tasks.

She did repeat experiments, and what she confirmed is that individuals of all ages remember twice as many uncompleted tasks as completed ones. The way that curiosity works into this is that when you pique curiosity, there's this trigger that goes off in your brain. It's a mental loop that just stays open. There's no conclusion to it.

With your prospects, if you open up a mental loop using some kind of curiosity, the only way to close it is if they can figure out the answer, whatever it is that's making them curious. And you can use this to your advantage.

Popular television programs do this all the time. They end the episode with something that piques your curiosity. They're not going to reveal it until the next episode, the next week. It gives you an incentive to tune in, because you can't turn off that mental loop they've opened. You can't turn it off until you get the answer to whatever the situation is that they presented that piqued your curiosity.

I do this quite a bit, and one of the best ways to do this is through bullets. You have bulleted copy, and going back to what you said earlier, Dale, bullets are something that makes copy very easy to read. You present information that's easily "scannable."

If you have people who are just looking through the copy and giving it an initial glance, looking for something that grabs their interest, bullets are like headlines. They grab interest and encourage people to keep on reading.

On a side note, that's the way that most people read online. Studies show that with websites, especially, people scan first looking for something that grabs their interest, and then they go back and read in more detail. And so bullets can do that.

Dale: It makes absolute sense. Curiosity is such a powerful, powerful tool. We've been talking about print and online ads, but I also write radio ads and again, the techniques we're talking about, the piquing of curiosity works not just for print, but it works for other broadcast mediums, too, like radio and television. Again, you're hitting the mark.

Tom: All sales-based decisions are based on emotions, and these carry over to whatever medium you use, whether it's radio, print, TV or another medium.

Let's move on to the third mistake. You may be thinking *My marketing should focus on my product or service*. Truthfully, it should not. It shouldn't focus on the actual product or service. Instead, it should focus on the end result, what your product or service will provide for people.

That's all people are worried about. We go back, again, to *What's in it for me*. There's something that your prospects want that your product or service can provide. It's not the actual product or service.

Let's use a lawnmower as an example. A prospect for a lawnmower just wants beautiful grass. They want cutting the grass to be easy. Now, if a toaster could cut the grass, then a prospect would want a toaster to do that job. They don't care what the medium is to make their yard beautiful. They don't really care how they get to that point.

Using your marketing to focus on your product or service is definitely a mistake. And this goes back to your headlines, as well. Your headline shouldn't be about your product or service. It should be about that end result.

Recently I was working on a piece and the original headline was "The new standard in high performance storage." We changed it to read, "The guaranteed easiest way to double your storage abilities, boost efficiency and slash your operating costs." So, we're taking it to the next level. We're giving people an end result with that storage device.

Dale: Absolutely. You need to focus on the solution that your product or service provides.

Once a year, our CEO gathers everyone into an auditorium to discuss our business strategy. One of the things he always says is, "Ladies and gentlemen, we don't sell financial services products. We sell solutions." You need to let people know that you have the solution for whatever their particular desire is.

It's all fine and good to tell people about the bells and whistles of the product, but the first thing you need to give them is the solution. How is it going to help them? Again, it goes back to the *What's in it for me* from the client's perspective.

Tom: It's great to hear that the CEO of a large organization is saying the same thing. Whether you're an entrepreneur or a Fortune 500 company, the outcome is still the same. The prospect still wants the same thing.

Dale: It tells you how valuable this information is that you're getting right now with this discussion. It really does work and it does have real-world implications. The proof is out there.

Tom: The fourth mistake is one I touched on a bit earlier, which is going for the sale immediately. This goes back to the mistake of thinking *What can I write, right now, that will get an instant sale* when you're developing a marketing piece.

Whether it's an ad or some other type of marketing piece (maybe it's just an e-mail that you're sending out), there will be instances where you're going to get an instant sale. That's great. That's like gravy.

In most cases, if your product costs more than $20, the likelihood of getting an instant sale from your marketing piece the first time a prospect sees it (unless they see it at the instant they are looking for that solution) is not very good.

Instead of trying to get the sale immediately, what I recommend is using your marketing pieces to start developing a list, because you're going to want to communicate with your prospects over and over again. You want to develop a relationship with prospects.

You don't want to be viewed as just a salesperson, because there aren't many people who enjoy sales pressure. However, if you can come across as someone who helps a prospect (say coming from an educational perspective where you're giving them knowledge they didn't have before), you will be viewed much differently than if you were somebody just trying to give them a high-pressure pitch.

When discussing this mistake, we have to talk about the two most critical elements in a marketing relationship. A marketing relationship is like a marriage. Imagine meeting your spouse on the first date and saying right at that moment, "Let's get married. I want to marry you now."

Of course, there are cases where people meet for the first time and they get married. But in most instances, it takes time to develop a relationship. And in a marketing relationship, the two most critical elements are *frequency of contact* and the *value of your communication*. You have to communicate with your prospects often, and you have to always give them something of value.

That's where list development comes into play. With a marketing piece, especially if you have a high-ticket item, you want to develop that relationship. You want to use your marketing piece to get your prospect to take one initial step, which is to provide an e-mail address for you to deliver more information, or to dial an (800) number so they can get information from a recorded call.

The key there is getting that prospect's contact information so you can continue the relationship. This is extremely powerful, because then you're not having to chase down prospects. Basically, you're having prospects raise their hands and tell you, "Yes, I'm interested in what you provide. Go ahead and send me more information." You've just created opportunity. They've opened up the door.

I'll give you an example. I am running an ad this month in a newspaper. In the ad, I make absolutely no effort to generate a sale. The only goal is to get prospects to raise their hands and ask me to deliver information to them. At the end of the ad, I have a call to action. I have them go to a website so they can receive a free report that talks about how to improve persuasion in their marketing materials.

Once people request that, then I know they're interested in that material, and I can follow up with additional e-mails or maybe a phone call. For me, most of the time it's through e-mails because it's more comfortable for people to get information, especially initially, without human interaction. I like to make it really easy for prospects to gather information knowing there is no pressure.

Dale: Tom, not necessarily going for the sale immediately is a great technique to use. My perspective from the corporate world is that, yes, this really works. One of the products our company offers is life insurance. Once a month, the company sends out an electronic newsletter with information about holidays and going back to school.

The point is, the newsletter provides helpful, free information. Over time, this e-newsletter is hopefully creating a relationship with the recipients who value that information. As that relationship develops, they become more familiar with our organization. In addition, the newsletters do have information about purchasing products. The electronic newsletter is one of the mediums that brings the customer to us to purchase products.

It really does work, so I would just remind our listeners and our readers that you don't need to go for the sale immediately. You really need to develop that relationship. Spend the time and effort to give them some valuable information, and you will be rewarded down the road.

Tom: It's great you bring that up, because you want the prospects to see you as someone who is educating them. You're just giving them good, valuable information. And that's a very different position to be in compared to somebody who is just a salesperson.

As a prospect, who would you prefer to get information from? Would you rather get information from an educator or somebody who is giving you that information for a sales pitch? That's an easy question to answer.

Dale: The answer is easy. I just purchased a new vehicle last month. Had the salesperson I purchased it through been going for the sale immediately, it would have been a total turnoff. He and I developed a relationship. I spent days asking about this particular van, everything from the tires to the heating and ventilation.

He was more than happy to give me the information and never conveyed any type of annoyance or irritability. He never actually went into the sales pitch until after three or four days of communication — face-to-face, e-mail, phone calls, text message. He was there to answer questions through all those mediums.

By the end of the fourth day, I was feeling comfortable enough with the van. It had everything we needed. The price was great. At that point, it was an easy sale for that particular salesperson.

Tom: That's an example of a high-ticket item. Yes, it takes extra effort and, if it's coming from an educational perspective, that effort is well worth the time. And from the perspective of the prospect, it makes the information you receive much more valuable.

Once they actually do the sales pitch, at that point, it's welcomed because they've already established that relationship with you. You know the sales pitch is coming, and you're expecting it. But at that point, it's okay because the relationship is already there.

Dale: Exactly. Had he come with a sales pitch right off the bat, I would have been off to the next car lot. You be the one who cuts through the clutter with timely, valuable information, develop the relationship, and they'll come back to you.

Tom: Let's go on to mistake #5, which is not doing something different than the competition. A lot of times I see marketing materials where the entire concept, or idea behind it, is basically just a copy of that company's competition.

There are some industries that do this more often than others. They'll see their competition does something (and it could be something as basic as just putting up a new website). Well, then the owner of the other company thinks *Oh, well, ABC Company just put up a new website. We better get a new one up there. We've got to do that, too.*

All they're doing is just copying what they already see in the marketplace, which is an incredible mistake because marketing is all about sticking out from the crowd and drawing attention to yourself. If you do what everybody else does, it's impossible for you to generate attention or interest. You're just blending into the background

There's not a whole lot I can say about this mistake. You must be willing to do something different and step out of your comfort zone. If you get an idea and your initial thought is *Boy, that seems a little bit off-the-wall*, oftentimes that's a good sign. Because if it's something that your competition is not doing and nobody in your industry is doing, it's going to attract attention.

Now, you can take ideas from other industries and apply those to your own industry. If you see an activity in another industry, but nobody's doing it in your industry, then it can be okay to try it out. You can always get ideas by watching the marketing in other industries, but it's a big mistake to copy marketing within your industry.

Another thing you can do to make you or your company a little bit different (and we've touched on this, but I just haven't phrased it this way) is to encourage interaction with your prospects. Many times in marketing pieces there's no encouragement to interact with prospects.

That's one way you can stand apart and do something a little bit different. Ultimately, people make buying decisions because they buy from people, not from companies or products. By encouraging interaction, you're doing something different. You're looking to develop that relationship with prospects. You're offering some type of availability that likely your competition is not doing.

There are not too many details I can give you on this. Just be willing to do something different. Step out-of-bounds. Do something that's going to draw attention to yourself.

Dale: Exactly. Differentiate yourself. Work outside of the box. Do what you've got to do to make yourself different from the pack.

Tom: The bottom line is many people have a fear factor. They think *What will people say if I do this?* Well, it's a good thing if your marketing piece gets people talking, because that's drawing attention to you. I'm sure you've heard that "even bad publicity is good publicity." There is some truth to that.

You don't want to do anything so outrageous that it goes beyond certain guidelines or ethical considerations. In most cases, when you do something that's different, it will not be viewed unfavorably. Just try to think outside the box a little bit. Don't be afraid to try something new, something different.

These days, many people think the only marketing medium is online advertising, running ads in newspapers, or maybe a Yellow Pages ad. Many people think that direct mail is dead. Well, that's a sign you may want to try it. If nobody in your industry is doing direct mail, imagine the attention you'll get by doing it. Just be willing to do something that's a little bit different.

Let's go on to #6. Number six is not addressing your prospects' concerns. When your prospects are reading your marketing materials, they go through a natural thought process. We've already discussed that they're thinking *What's in it for me?* But there are other questions that they'll have depending on what your content says.

With any type of marketing piece, you want to make sure you're targeting the right prospects. Every person is not a prospect for your business, regardless of what industry you're in. Your best prospects are the ones who have problems you can solve.

When writing your content, you should have a pretty good idea of what your prospects are thinking at the time. There are certain questions those prospects are going to have while reading your copy, and you need to address those. If you don't, you are risking your prospects' readership. They're going to stop reading, if their questions aren't getting answered while reading your copy.

I'll give you an example. Just today, I was working on some copy for a local business club. The club started off strong with monthly meetings, but then it slowly fizzled out. The copy I was working on was for a re-launch of this club. The promotion is going out to previous attendees.

Since we're going to promote to people who attended these meetings, naturally, when they receive this promotional material, they are going to wonder *What happened last year? Why did it stop? Why is it re-launching now?*

You have to address that. If you know they're thinking that, you've have to respond. Don't leave them guessing. If you leave them guessing, they're not going to read anymore. There's really no reason for them to attend, because they've got this question and there's a negative feeling associated with it.

As you read your own writing, try thinking from a prospect's perspective. What are they thinking after they read that? Do they have some concerns? Do they have some questions? Just make sure you address that in the copy. It doesn't necessarily have to be immediately after, but it has to be very early on. It is important you answer potential doubts and questions early in a marketing piece.

Dale: Tom, you touched on this a little bit. Another reason to address all the questions your prospect may have is if you don't answer the questions, they're going to come up with their own answers. At that point, you're at the mercy of whatever they happen to be thinking. If it's something negative, well, unfortunately perception becomes reality in that case and you don't want that to happen.

Tom: And that's so incredibly dangerous. I know in some pieces — I can think of some sales letters, in particular — I've come out and said, "At this point, I'm sure you have several questions, so let's go ahead and address those." And I will list the questions out, almost as if it's a Q&A. I'll list the question and then provide a response.

For instance, a lot of times in a sales letter, price is something people have concerns about, so you have to address that. You've have to say, "You may view the price as being a little too high." Or it may be too low. And if it's too low, "Here's why I'm providing this product or service at this price right now. Here's why you're getting this incredible value."

And that brings up another point. When people have concerns over price, it's not always because something is priced too high. It also happens if something is priced too low. They may feel like they're not getting enough value if they buy something that's cheap. *Is it cheaply made?* You've got to address that.

Let's move on to #7, and Dale, I know we've discussed this one at length many times. This is one that is really important. Prospects might get all the way through your piece, but if you don't have this one element, then often you're not going to get a sale or even an inquiry. And that mistake is no *call to action.*

A marketing piece that doesn't have a call to action is basically an invisible marketing piece, because you make it impossible for people to respond to your marketing message. They don't know what to do.

Dale: It's a huge mistake.

Tom: You mentioned this in the last mistake. If you leave it up to your prospects to make a decision, that becomes really dangerous because you don't know what they're going to do. You have to be incredibly clear on the next step they should take. And, you have to tell them.

If you want your prospect to dial a phone number with their left index finger and then put the receiver to their right ear, then tell them to do that. Obviously, that's an exaggeration, but you have to be incredibly clear on what you want them to do.

Then take it a step further, and tell them what's going to happen after they take that step. You don't even leave the door open as to what's going to happen next. They need an incredibly clear picture of what's going to occur if they take your call to action.

Dale: And I cannot stress enough the importance of the call to action. If you don't have a call to action at the end of your marketing piece, no matter *what* you're doing — whether you're selling a product, whether you're a human resources recruiter looking for people to join your organization — you need to make it clear what you want them to do.

As Tom said, if you want them to call a toll-free number and then hit a particular option once they hear the voice prompt, the tell them to do that. Do you want them to go to a website? Do you want them to come to a seminar? Whatever it is, be extremely, extremely clear and diligent in telling them what you want them to do.

Imagine you write this marketing piece. You spend money on the design. It's in full color and everything is wonderful. You've written a great headline. You have bullet points and all of the techniques we've discussed. Then the end *has no call to action.*

That's like getting the instructions to go someplace from *MapQuest*, but the last step is missing. You've been guided all the way to the end, and you never actually get to where you need to go. It's just a futile effort. You are throwing money away if you don't include that call to action.

Tom: Like you said, this has to be on every marketing piece. Even if it's a simple e-mail going out to a single person, you have to tell that person what you want them to do. Don't leave it up to them to make that decision. You want to make the call to action as specific as possible, just as you touched on, Dale. Don't forget it, and make that next step really obvious.

I see this mistake a lot with ads. An example I can think of immediately is *Google AdWords*. You see people run ads and they have a call to action like "Go to … " and they'll list their website. Say they're giving away a special report. Once you're at that website, you can't figure out what the call to action is. They told you to go there to get a free report, but you can't find where the free report is.

Whatever your call to action is, make it clear. Then once they take that step, make sure your prospects know they've taken the right step. Also, make it clear they know what's going to happen next after they take that step.

Mistake #8 is a widespread mistake. It's something I don't think needs an incredible amount of attention, although it is very important. And that is focusing too much on your company logo or company name. This kind of ties in with mistake #3, which is making your product or service the focus of your marketing message.

Many times I see companies that make the focus of their marketing piece their logo or company name. The truth is, your prospects could care less about your logo or your company name. Now, a lot of times in ads for well-known companies, you'll see a big focus on a company name, say like Coke or Amazon.com. Well, those companies have huge budgets and brand recognition that they've built up over time.

In the case of most small business owners and entrepreneurs, you do not have the brand recognition. You also don't have the budget that allows you to constantly put your company name or your logo in front of people over and over again.

The example I like using is Super Bowl commercials. There is incredible money spent by companies just on creative commercials so they can get their name out there. Yet, a lot of times you'll remember the commercial, but you have no idea which company it was or what the product or service is that they provide. That is an incredible waste of money.

Smart marketing focuses more on the solution and the end result. That's what your prospects are concerned about. They don't really care how much you spend on your logo. If you spent thousands on your logo, you may think you need to give it prominent placement in your marketing materials. But that's just a waste of money, especially in an ad. You're wasting space.

Instead, use that prominent space at the top for a headline that's going to explain what your prospects are going to get by continuing to read your marketing piece, as well as the solution you can provide. In most cases, a company name does not describe the solution your product or service can provide. So it's a big, big mistake if you're using your company name or your logo as the focal point of your marketing piece.

Dale: Yes, and over time, that familiarity is only achieved through an engaging message, a good headline, and a call to action. When those are done appropriately, the familiarity will come with your logo and company name.

Tom: I talked earlier about the ad I'm running this month, and basically the call to action is just to get people to download this free report. I think a lot of people would be surprised that this ad does not include my company name or logo. The ad is pure text, because all I'm looking to do is deliver information of value to prospects.

I believe most prospects don't care what your company name is. If they're getting value, it wouldn't matter if my company name was Smith Jones, Inc. or Write Way Solutions.

Dale: Absolutely. The customers will come looking for you through your company name or logo after you've provided that service. The familiarity will come.

Tom: Mistake #9 is targeting the wrong prospects. You just can't think of your prospects as being anybody. Regardless of what business you're in, not every person is a prospect for your product or service.

Drilling a little deeper into this, I hear this mistake quite a bit from prospects who contact me. A lot of times they will contact me about writing an ad. I've heard this many, many times.

People will tell me they want to run an ad in a publication, and they'll tell me the name of the publication. My first question is, "Is your target audience reading that publication?" A lot of times, their response will be, "Well, it's really cheap to get in there. It's only going to cost me 'X' dollars to get my ad in."

Well, the cost doesn't really matter. You can spend $10 or you can spend $10,000. If your prospects aren't reading that publication or aren't looking at that publication, your money is just wasted.

You can spend $10,000 on an ad, but if you get $100,000 from that ad because that ad is in a publication that reaches your target audience, then that's a great investment. If you spend $10 on an ad and your publication isn't getting in front of your audience, then you're throwing away 10 bucks.

In the grand scheme of things, would you rather lose 10 bucks or spend $10,000 and get $100,000 back? The investment in the second opportunity is minimal when you consider the profit you would make.

The key is don't think of your prospects as every single person. Target the right prospects. Think about your business and who has delivered the biggest gains for your business. Who results in the most revenue? Then find those people and target those people.

You then can develop a list for your marketing materials of those people who will naturally come to you, and will raise their hand for your information. Then you can continue to market to them over and over.

In effect, if you're targeting the right prospects with your marketing, you'll start attracting the right prospects. I'm not talking about attracting as in the movie *The Secret*. I'm talking about not having to go after them. They're going to find your information, volunteer themselves as your prospects, and ask for your information. Once they do that, you can continue to market to them.

And when you have your own list, it's very inexpensive to do that. How much does it cost to send an e-mail, if you have an e-mail list? A minimal amount. If you pair that with a traditional ad, it can be very inexpensive. So definitely target those right prospects so they start finding you.

Dale: If I may, let me give you an extreme, real-world example related to what you mentioned earlier about the pitfalls of picking a certain advertising medium just because it's cheap.

I work in a city right on the Ohio River in the Midwest, and there are a lot of one-way streets because it's a very old city. There's a billboard on the street where I work, which literally faces the wrong way on a one-way street. I can just imagine that when an advertiser who is looking to buy this billboard space sees the rate on it, they think, "Oh, my goodness. What a great deal!"

What they don't realize is, literally, this billboard faces the wrong way on a one-way street. So drivers are coming up on it and seeing the back of it. The only way they're ever going to read this billboard is if they're reading things over their shoulder or through the rearview mirror in their cars.

Just think about the medium you're using. Just because it's cut-rate advertising doesn't mean it's effective. Don't be lulled into that mistake. You may be purchasing a billboard that faces the wrong way on a one-way street.

Tom: Now that's a real-world example. It's hard to imagine that happening. That's incredible.

Let's move on to mistake #10. Mistake #10 is not backing up your claims with proof. This is a mistake I see over and over again. You see in marketing pieces where a company makes outrageous claims. People will read them, and their first thought is *That's outrageous.* Well, it wouldn't be as outrageous if you just backed up the claim.

Very common claims are "We're the leading provider of 'X'" in a specific region or "We're the #1 seller of vacuums in Phoenix." You see simple claims like those all the time, but there's no proof backing up those claims. Any claim or fact that you're using in your marketing materials should be backed up because you have to prove it.

People are naturally cautious and skeptical. You have to show them that what you're claiming is actually true. You want to use things like testimonials or case studies where people can actually read information. If it's a video, people should be able to watch information about people just like them who had their problem solved using the solution you provide.

Statistics. Make a claim and back it up with statistics. And one quick note about statistics. You want to be very specific with statistics. Something like "We've served more than 100,000 people in Phoenix" is simply too vague. When you're specific, your facts become more believable. You want to be as specific as possible.

Another way you can back up claims is you can demonstrate your product or service in use. If you say your product or service can do something, well then demonstrate it. And this is a great technique you can take from infomercials.

Regardless of your views on infomercials, they're incredibly effective and they are big money-makers. And one of the big techniques used in infomercials is demonstrations. You may not believe the testimonials or even the demonstration, but the fact is they're taking steps to demonstrate that product in action to increase their credibility with you and to target your skepticism.

That's something you can use in any product or service. Just demonstrate that product or service in use. And in a way, case studies or testimonials are a way of demonstrating your product, especially if you're providing a service.

Sometimes it can be a little bit difficult to demonstrate a service. But if you have a testimonial that describes a common problem your prospect had, how you started to work with them, how you changed the problem, and then how their life is different now, well, that is a way of demonstrating your service.

The final way you can back up a claim with proof (and I touched on this one earlier) is encourage involvement. We've all heard the term "snake oil salesman." They come with a quick solution and then they leave town.

Well, when you encourage interaction, you prove to your prospects that you're here for the long haul. You're here because you really do care about what you're providing, and that you are available. This helps address your prospect's skepticism.

Any thoughts on that mistake, Dale?

Dale: Can I go back to the testimonials and statistics again? Let me talk about a pet peeve of mine here. If you're going to use a testimonial in your outreach, be as specific as possible. And by that, what I mean is (of course with their permission) give the name of the person who is providing the testimonial.

I believe that testimonials lose all credibility when it's just something very generic like two initials. The two initials of the first and last name might as well be "B.S." In the consumer's mind, if the person didn't put their entire name on there, or worse, if you're not confident enough in that testimonial that you don't print the entire name, it does nothing but put doubt in the consumer's mind.

Tom: Dale, that is such a great point. I can't stress that enough, either. It's so true. You see those types of testimonials quite a bit and, honestly, you just wonder why people still do that anymore. I don't think anybody believes those.

A lot of times you'll see testimonials that are really vague, like "This product was great, and I would definitely use it again." Oftentimes, they just make up the testimonials. Be specific with your testimonials.

Talk about a situation a person was in, explain how you solved that problem and then what the situation was. It makes the testimonial more believable.

Mistake #11 found in marketing materials is not having a deadline. I wish more companies included deadlines in their marketing pieces.

The problem is that if you leave it up to prospects to make a decision on when they will take action, a lot of times they will just wait. And we know the longer the wait, the less likely it is they will take action. That's just a natural human reaction. But when you include deadlines, then you encourage a quick reaction, quick involvement and a quick response. Deadlines can be very effective.

Sometimes including a deadline with a marketing piece will increase your response rate, because there is this added urgency. Probably the most common deadline is asking for a response by "X" date to get whatever it is that you offer. But you can also say there's a limited number of items available or state there's a limited period of time in which they can respond.

The main thing, though, with your deadline, is you have to be honest with it. You lose all credibility if you make a deadline and then you don't stick to it. People know it isn't legitimate, and then the deadline in your next marketing piece becomes ineffective. Just be honest with your deadlines.

Dale: A deadline is effective because it creates urgency with your prospect, and when there's urgency created, there's also priority created.

Tom: Good point. The next mistake is not reversing the risk for your prospects. The easiest way to reverse risk for your prospects is to include some kind of a guarantee. If you're truly confident in your product or service and the solution it provides, then you need to back it up. You need to prove to your prospects that you're so confident in it that you will take all the risk.

The most common are 30-day guarantees or 60-day guarantees. Whatever it may be, give some kind of guarantee where it reverses the risk. That way you make it very easy for your prospects, customers or clients to respond — and you make it comfortable for them. If they're uncomfortable, they're not going to respond or even continue reading.

But when you have a guarantee — when you back up your claim or your offer — and you put all the risk on yourself, then you show confidence in whatever you provide and you eliminate risk, which makes it very easy for your prospects to respond.

Dale: Absolutely. The guarantee will go a long way with those prospects. You couldn't have said it any better, Tom.

Tom: I'm going to quickly go through all the mistakes we've mentioned because the final two are more formatting mistakes.

- Mistake # 1 is having the copy focus too much on *we, our*, and the *company name*.
- Mistake #2 is having no headline.
- Mistake #3 is making your product or service the focus of your marketing message.
- Mistake #4 is going for the sale immediately and not developing a list.
- Mistake #5 is being afraid to do something different.
- Mistake #6 is not addressing your prospects' concerns.
- Mistake #7 is not having a call to action.
- Mistake #8 is focusing too much on your logo or company name.
- Mistake #9 is targeting the wrong prospects.
- Mistake #10 is not backing up claims with proof.
- Mistake #11 is not having a deadline.
- Mistake #12 is not reversing the risk for your prospects to take action.

I want to finish up here with two more mistakes which have to do with formatting that can reduce readership. You want to stay away from these when putting together your marketing piece or having your designer format your marketing.

Mistake #13 is having too much reverse font. Reverse font is when you have a light-colored font with a dark background. The reason that this is a mistake is because it makes your copy very difficult to read.

Go back to newspapers, magazines and books, and how the eyes are naturally used to reading a white or off-white background with a black font. Most of the materials we read have a light background and a dark font. That's simply what we're used to.

I'm not saying can't use reverse font in your marketing materials, but use it sparingly. It can be effective if you have a short headline to attract attention. But the bulk of your copy should use a dark font and a light background.

I'm sure you've seen it before, Dale, where you have these long paragraphs of text. The background may be like dark blue or even black. And when that font is small, it causes strain on the eyes. That's going to reduce readership. If a reader's eyes are straining, they're going to stop because it's uncomfortable.

Dale, do you have any experience with that one?

Dale: Absolutely. I have a recent example. I was doing a search on Steven Hawking, the physicist. Believe it or not, I got to a website about his work and the entire website was in reverse font. I couldn't believe it. It strained my eyes so much that I probably read the first four sentences of the website, and I couldn't go on.

There was a wealth of information on there, but I couldn't read anything else. The strain on my eyes was to the point where it actually was uncomfortable. I just can't believe that a web designer put that together and somebody approved it. It's one of the quickest ways to turn your prospects off.

It's okay in minimal to small doses, like you said, for a headline. I've see that in print plenty of times, and truth be told, we sometimes employ that in the organization I work for. But, it's used very minimally and by far, your best bet is to use a light-colored background with a dark font.

White space is a good thing. White space is when you have a dark font on a white background and plenty of white space around it. It's easiest for people to read, and it's not overwhelming.

Tom: You touched on it. This problem is rampant on the Internet. There are so many websites, and you see it a lot of times with blogs, as well, where you have the reverse font. On something like a blog where it's all posts in text, it's amazing how just reading can really cause a strain and even cause pain for some people. It's a simple mistake to fix. Make sure your font is dark with a light background.

The final mistake is something that we touched on several times, but I just want to stress it again. This goes along with making your copy easy to read and is related to the reverse font. That is, long paragraphs, long blocks of text and long sentences.

As we've repeated throughout, you have to make things easy on your prospects. One way to prevent readership from being a chore for your prospects is to make sure your copy is inviting to read.

So you have a headline. Then you might have a sentence and a short paragraph so that it's naturally flowing. Use bullets and that kind of stuff, too. Large blocks of text are very intimidating and, from a reader perspective, it looks like a lot of work to get through. You don't want your marketing piece to look like a textbook, where it's just going to be work for your prospects to get through it.

Now this may go against what your English teacher taught you back in high school. You often hear you don't want one-sentence paragraphs, phrases or word fragments.

Well, if you're really writing your copy as if it's a conversation, you will have instances where you have one-sentence paragraphs and incredibly short sentences. You may even have single-word paragraphs.

I use single-word paragraphs a lot. I also often use fragments and end them with an ellipsis. An ellipsis is just the three dots that tell you the thought continues. It's a way to get your prospects to the next sentence … to keep them going.

A fragment in a sentence will also trigger curiosity. You're thinking *What's next? What am I missing* — so you keep on reading. There are times where things like fragments will be effective in a marketing piece. Obviously, you don't want to use the tactic over and over again, because then it loses its effectiveness. But an occasional fragment or maybe a one-word paragraph or sentence is fine.

The main idea is to make copy that's very easy to read. Keep your paragraphs short. My guideline, a lot of times, is 2-4 lines. Now I'm not saying 2-4 sentences per paragraph — 2-4 *lines*. That's just a short block of text that makes it easy for a reader to comprehend.

Once you start getting beyond that, it becomes a little more difficult. What do you think, Dale?

Dale: Absolutely. It goes back to that motto I said during the previous tip, which is "White space is good." One of the graphic designers in my work area has a little card in her cubicle, and it says, "White space is good." This also refers to the idea of keeping your paragraphs short and succinct. When you keep them short and succinct, it's not as intimidating and overwhelming or as oppressive to the reader.

The white space comes when you provide information in bite-sized chunks, maybe 2-4 lines. Maybe it's just bullet points. But the more white space people see and the less text they see, the better your chances of the prospect reading through everything.

Tom: Excellent, and I think it's time to wrap up.

With all these mistakes, you just have to think from a prospect's perspective. That's the theme I want to get across the most with the mistakes we talked about today. You just have to change your focus. It's not about you or your company. All the solutions to the mistakes we addressed today make readership and response much easier for your prospects.

We'll wrap this up. Dale, I just want to thank you for your time as well as your insights. You really do offer a valuable and unique perspective for the listeners. You're from the corporate world and a Fortune 500 company. What I'm offering, a lot of times, is coming from that small business or the entrepreneurial mindset.

Here we've been able to combine both perspectives, and I think this is very valuable for people. They can see these mistakes carry over, regardless of who you target, what type of business you offer, or what industry you're in.

Dale: And the vast majority of the tips don't just carry over from industry to industry or from your small business to your large corporation. They also carry over to the nonprofit world. It also carries over from print to radio to TV broadcasts to the Internet. Whatever the medium, these basic fundamental tips that Tom provided are valuable, no matter how you apply them.

Tom: Again, Dale, thank you for the time. And for everyone who is listening to this or reading the transcript, I want to encourage you to become involved. If you have additional questions or any concerns about the mistakes we discussed, and how they apply to your business, don't hesitate to contact me. My number is (602) 305-6755 or you can contact me by e-mail at tom@writewaysolutions.com.

Here's What to Do Next ...

The strategies revealed in this book work. In fact, now that you've seen the other side of the marketing game, you'll begin noticing these ideas in action.

You now have a choice. There's no reason you can't succeed at elevating your marketing above the promotional garbage dumped on us every day. All you need is the desire to do something different.

So what's holding you back?

You just invested your most valuable asset — time — reading this book. Your decisions after closing the cover will determine your return on that investment.

Imagine what's possible with the new weapons in your marketing arsenal ...

Imagine attracting leads, instead of always chasing after them. Imagine establishing yourself as the go-to authority in your industry. Imagine spending less money (and effort) to get your message in front of larger audiences.

The map to get you there is in your hands. You just have to use it.

In the remaining pages, you'll find several bonus resources (including links to exclusive audio interviews with marketing experts and a $145 Copy Critique Certificate) to help steer you in the right direction. But before giving them to you, I have a favor to ask.

If you found value in what you just read and believe the insight I shared could help another business owner or entrepreneur, could you please go back to Amazon.com or wherever you

bought this book and leave a review? As you know, reviews help get books in front of new readers.

Of course, after you leave your review, please let me know so I can post your praises (or criticism) on my refrigerator. I'd really like to prove to my wife that I'm doing something useful with all these hours clicking on a keyboard.

Good luck and thank you for sharing your time with me. Please keep me updated on your progress.

Tom Trush
E-mail: tom@writewaysolutions.com
Twitter: @tomtrush
Facebook: http://www.facebook.com/tomtrush

Part V: **Marketing Tips Review & Resources**

- When put in front of the wrong audience, even the most persuasive marketing messages get ignored.

- Don't forget the clients/customers who haven't done business with you in some time. They deserve your marketing attention, too.

- Why wait around for someone to designate you as an expert? Grab that tile today — it's your position! You don't need a large audience ... you don't need a big budget ... you don't need any special equipment or training. You just need the guts to give advice, share what you know and demonstrate why you are an authority.

- The most successful marketers (and business professionals, for that matter) live with fear because they do things every day that few people are willing to try.

- You are not the only person who has bombed on a marketing campaign. Failures in marketing are part of the process — they happen to everyone. You only fail when you give up trying.

- There's no rule against including more than your name, title, company name and contact phone/e-mail on your business card. Add an irresistible free offer so you can collect names and e-mail addresses to grow your prospect list.

- You can't let your prospects wait — give them what they want now. When you give prospects immediate access to beneficial information focused on them, you get rewarded with action.

- All elements of your marketing piece should be designed to do one thing and one thing only — get prospects to read the first sentence of copy. After the first sentence, your objective is to move them to the second sentence. When prospects finish the second sentence, you must convince them to read the third sentence ... fourth sentence ... fifth sentence ... and so on.

- Don't be afraid to admit mistakes in your marketing materials, especially when they involve issues your prospects can relate to.

- Who doesn't like being part of a select group? While everyone else trumpets "me too" promises, your limited-time offer, special privileges or members-only invitations offer your prospects access to something others only wish they had.

- Who are you more likely to take advice from — a trusted friend or a corporate figurehead? Communicate with your prospects and clients like they're friends.

- Most marketing doesn't work because it targets broad audiences of people who will never buy. You're better off using your marketing to qualify your prospects, follow up with consistent communication to establish credibility and trust, and then go after a sale.

- Embrace your harshest critics — they are a sure sign you're doing something right.

- Your chance at a sale hinges on your ability to transform what you offer into benefits your prospects understand. Confuse your audience and they'll go searching for a message they can comprehend — and you probably won't see them again.

- Even the best marketing ideas fail when not implemented.

- Your prospects are afraid of the unknown. If you don't clearly communicate what happens after moving forward with your offer, then your prospects are less likely to respond. So use your writing to help them visualize what it's like to work with you or use your product or service.

- Pushing your message in front of people who have not expressed interest in what you offer is not marketing — it's hoping.

- Far too many opportunities get missed on marketing materials because prospects don't know what step to take next. If you want your prospects to do something, then you must give them direction.

- These days, lofty promises and fabricated facts get thrown around like rice at a wedding. Prove all claims mentioned in your marketing materials.

- When you have your own prospect list, you can use e-mail to test new ideas, promote products or services and drive traffic to your website whenever you want. Start building your list today.

- The two most critical elements in a marketing relationship are the frequency of your interaction and the value of your communication. Simply put, you must contact your prospects often and give them information they view as valuable.

- Your company name and logo have zero effect on the outcome you can provide for your prospects. So don't make either one the focal point of your ads or marketing pieces.

- The mind "thinks" in images, not words. So use your text to paint a picture of your product or service in action and the end result it offers to your prospects. Work in fears, agitate pains and then promise a better life in some way.

- Write your marketing copy as if you're talking to a single prospect — not a group of people.

- If you want your marketing to deliver different results, you must be willing to do something different.

- Promote the benefits of your product or service. Facts about your product or service are features, while benefits explain how those facts positively affect your prospects.

- Your prospects flee to your competitors the instant they don't see value in your content. Marketers who provide the most value win.

- Don't hesitate to share knowledge. Your prospects don't have the same experience as you. So even if you deliver exact instructions on how they can solve their problem, there's little chance your prospects will do it correctly or have the desire to try.

- You can't create desire where none exists — you can only deepen a desire that's already present. Trying to convince people they need your product or service puts you in an impossible position for marketing success.

- People are likely to pay more for cures than they will for preventions.

- If you're not using your marketing to establish yourself as the authority in your industry, you're doing something wrong.

- Demonstrate your product or service by using words that create mental images in your prospects' minds — and back up your claims with proof.

- Taking a single stab at any random marketing activity will only leave you frustrated, especially if you don't see instant results. Understand consistency is critical to marketing success. You'll experience exponential benefits when you market on a regular basis — not just when you're desperate for clients.

- Get your prospects involved in your marketing message. Present self-tests, offer free tools and post videos with insight that keeps people coming back to you.

- Your prospects are more easily persuaded when you use the exact words they use to describe the problem you solve.

- The currency in today's marketing world is no longer money — it's information. As you share more information, your status as an authority soars.

- Your prospects don't only look for solutions in one location — they gather information from a variety of sources. Like any smart financial investment, effective marketing involves spreading out your risk using a variety of mediums to reach your target audience.

- If you don't know your prospects' problems, you'll have a tough time writing anything that grabs their attention. So before you sit in front of your keyword or put pen to paper, you need a vivid picture of what keeps your target audience awake at night.

- Use your marketing copy to promote the outcome — not the process for getting there.

- Look at most small business marketing copy, and you'll notice a dangerous trend — the message is all about the company or the people who work there. Frequent uses of the words "we," "our" or the company name are an immediate giveaway. The problem with this type of ego-based message is it offers little benefit to prospects. You'll never persuade potential customers to loosen the choke-hold on their wallets if all you do is talk about yourself. After all, your prospects are only concerned about their own needs and desires.

- Don't market your product or service. Instead, explain to your prospects the end results (or solutions) they'll experience as a result of your product or service.

- Figure out how your prospects feel. Are they frustrated, scared or confused? Do they feel guilty? Are they insecure about their situation? Once you know these answers, add to your marketing materials the exact words your prospects use to describe their feelings. Taking this step helps prove to your prospects you understand them because you "speak" their language.

- Make yourself known to the media as someone who shares knowledge. Pay attention to writers/editors who cover topics related to your industry and volunteer yourself as a source. You can contact them or regularly send out press releases that describe tips or strategies you can offer to their audiences.

- Purchasing decisions are not based on occupations, company names, logo designs, mission statements or the number of abbreviations after your name. Look around, however, and you'll see plenty of self-centered marketing messages focused on these items. Prospects hunt for people who can solve their problems. The more your marketing message focuses on your prospects' nagging needs, the more likely you'll receive responses. So showcase your expertise by offering information that details solutions.

- If your prospects don't know you or your company, or they view your product or service as being just like your competition's offering, you must educate before you pitch. This approach requires frequent interaction and more copy.

- Opinions are not a valid predictor of marketing success.

- Don't hesitate to do something different in your marketing. When you copy your competitors' strategies, you instantly level the playing field. As such, you may as well stop marketing altogether because it becomes impossible to secure space in your prospects' minds — you offer nothing on which they can base a buying a decision.

- You have the ability to deliver unlimited value to your prospects by giving them information that helps address their problems related to your product or service. In turn, each time you share your knowledge, you further establish yourself as an authority in your industry.

Exclusive Audio Interviews

Social Media Strategies That Silence Skeptics
- Interview with Rev. Alan Rudnick, pastor at the First Baptist Church of Ballston Spa
- Go to: http://www.writewaysolutions.com/blog/1442/social-media-strategies-that-silence-skeptics/

How to Create Predictable Profits for Your Business
- Interview with Charles Gaudet, founder and CEO of Predictable Profits
- Go to: http://www.writewaysolutions.com/blog/1330/how-to-create-predictable-profits-for-your-business/

How to Become Your Industry's Obvious Expert
- Interview with Stuart Selbst, owner of Stuart Selbst Consulting
- Go to: http://www.writewaysolutions.com/blog/1183/how-to-become-your-industrys-obvious-expert/

The Forgotten Facts You Must Never Overlook When Self-Publishing Your Book
- Interview with Nate Kuiper, owner of Compass Book
- Go to: http://www.writewaysolutions.com/blog/991/the-forgotten-facts-you-must-never-overlook-when-self-publishing-your-book/

How to Apply the Unconventional Marketing Tactics of a Teenage Super Affiliate to Your Business
- Interview with Joshua Elizetxe, digital marketing genius and serial entrepreneur
- Go to: http://www.writewaysolutions.com/blog/819/how-to-apply-the-unconventional-marketing-tactics-of-a-teenage-super-affiliate-to-your-business/

The Secrets of Advertising Psychology That Make Selling Simple
- Interview with Drew Eric Whitman, direct-response copywriter, consultant and author of *Cashvertising*
- Go to: http://www.writewaysolutions.com/blog/344/the-secrets-of-advertising-psychology-that-make-selling-simple/

Marketing Tips for Small Businesses Struggling to Survive
- Interview with Jon Ward, nationally acclaimed marketing and branding consultant
- Go to: http://www.writewaysolutions.com/blog/223/marketing-tips-for-small-businesses-struggling-to-survive/

How to Get Started Using Online Video to Promote Your Business
- Interview with Mike Koenigs, Internet marketer and online video expert
- Go to: http://www.writewaysolutions.com/blog/201/how-to-get-started-using-online-video-to-promote-your-business/

Are You Making These Mistakes on Your Website?
- Interview with Andy Renk, co-founder of Click for Clients
- Go to: http://www.writewaysolutions.com/blog/166/are-you-making-these-mistakes-on-your-website/

$145 Copy Critique Certificate

This Copy Critique Certificate entitles possessor to submit any single piece of copy – advertisement, e-mail, postcard, press release, brochure, web page or similar promotional material – for critique by Tom Trush.

_____   _____
                    Name   Date

Send Copy Critique Certificate, materials and
contact information to Tom at:
tom@writewaysolutions.com (include "Copy Critique" in subject line)
or
fax to 602.606.7920

After personally reviewing your materials, Tom will give you specific recommendations on how to modify your marketing piece for increased responses. You'll get a list of action steps to help position you as an industry authority, deliver higher returns on your marketing investments and allow you to reach larger audiences with less effort.

Terms and Conditions

Copy Critique Certificate expires 12 months from date of purchase. Please allow up to 10 business days for Tom's response. Consultation is delivered by e-mail only. Phone consultations can be scheduled – fees quoted on request. Finished materials or "rough drafts" for planned marketing materials can be submitted. This certificate is only redeemable for listed services.

All copy sent to Tom is kept confidential.

Bibliography

Burg, Bob and Mann, John David. *It's Not About You: A Little Story About What Matters Most in Business.* New York, NY: Penguin Group, 2011.

Caples, John. *Tested Advertising Methods.* Paramus, NJ: Prentice Hall, 1997 (5th ed.).

Cialdini, Robert. *Influence: The Psychology of Persuasion.* New York, NY: HarperCollins, 1998.

Edwards, Ray. *Writing Riches: Learn How to Boost Profits, Drive Sales and Master Your Financial Destiny with Results-Based Copy.* Garden City, NY: Morgan James Publishing, 2010.

Frank, Milo O. *How to Get Your Point Across in 30 Seconds or Less.* New York, NY: Pocket Books, 1986.

Frank, Stephanie. *The Accidental Millionaire: Leaping From Chance to Mastery in the Game of Life.* Scottsdale, AZ: Green Light Publishing, 2005.

Garber, Craig. *How to Make Maximum Money With Minimum Customers.* Lutz, FL: kingofcopy.com, 2009.

Garland, David Siteman. *Smarter, Faster, Cheaper: Non-Boring, Fluff-Free Strategies for Marketing and Promoting Your Business*. Hoboken, NJ: John Wiley & Sons, 2011.

Glazer, Bill. *Outrageous Advertising That's Outrageously Successful*. New York, NY: Glazer-Kennedy Publishing, 2009.

Hopkins, Claude. *My Life in Advertising*. Lincolnwood, IL: NTC Business Books, 1986, 1966.

Hopkins, Claude. *Scientific Advertising*. Lincolnwood, IL: NTC Business Books, 1986, 1966.

Kennedy, Dan. *No B.S. Direct Marketing*. Entrepreneur Press, 2006.

Krakowski, Sandi. *Read Their Mind: How to Hear What the Marketplace Wants & Build a Huge Business*. A Real Changed International, 2011.

Lindstrom, Martin. *Brandwashed: Tricks Companies Use to Manipulate Our Minds and Persuade Us to Buy*. New York, NY: Crown Publishing Group, 2011.

Morgan, John. *Brand Against the Machine: How to Build Your Brand, Cut Through the Marketing Noise, and Stand Out from the Competition*. Hoboken, NJ: John Wiley & Sons, Inc., 2011.

Nicholas, Ted. *Billion Dollar Marketing Secrets: How to Get a Massive Bang for Your Marketing Buck Online and Offline*. Indian Rocks Beach, FL: Ted Nicholas Direct, 2008.

Ogilvy, David. *Ogilvy on Advertising*. New York, NY: Vintage Books, 1983.

Schwartz, Eugene. *Breakthrough Advertising*. Bottom Line Books, 2004.

Scott, David Meerman. *The New Rules of Marketing & PR*. Hoboken, NJ: John Wiley & Sons, 2011.

Scott, David Meerman. *Newjacking: How to Inject Your Ideas Into a Breaking News Story and Generate Tons of Media Coverage.* Hoboken, NJ: John Wiley & Sons, 2012.

Stevens, Mark. *Your Marketing Sucks.* New York, NY: Three Rivers Press, 2005.

Sugarman, Joe. *The Adweek Copywriting Handbook.* Hoboken, NJ: John Wiley & Sons, 2007.

Vee, Jimmy. Miller, Travis. Bauer, Joel. *Gravitational Marketing: The Science of Attracting Customers.* Hoboken, NJ: John Wiley & Sons, 2008.

Vitale, Joe. *Buying Trances: A New Psychology of Sales and Marketing.* Hoboken, NJ: John Wiley & Sons, 2007.

Vitale, Joe. *Hypnotic Writing: How to Seduce and Persuade Customers with Only Your Words.* Hoboken, NJ: John Wiley & Sons, 2007.

Wheeler, Elmer. *Tested Sentences That Sell.* Englewood Cliffs, NJ: Prentice Hall, 1937.

Whitman, Drew Eric. *Cashvertising: How to Use More Than 100 Secrets of Ad-Agency Psychology to Make Big Money Selling Anything to Anyone.* Franklin Lakes, NJ: Career Press, 2009.

About Tom Trush

A direct-response copywriter and founder of Write Way Solutions in Phoenix, Arizona, Tom Trush helps business owners and entrepreneurs develop lead-capturing marketing materials. In addition to working with clients across the globe, Tom shares his educational approach to marketing at seminars and workshops, as well as in his own information products.

He firmly believes you can't go wrong in your marketing when you show compassion and a desire for helping people.

Tom's articles regularly appear in print publications, sales literature and on several online sites, including the *American Express OPEN Forum*, *Lawyer Marketing Alert* and *Alltop*. He is also the author of ***The Reluctant Writer's Guide to Creating Powerful Marketing Materials: 61 Easy Ideas to Attract Prospects and Get More Customers***.

Get more direct-response copywriting and marketing tips from Tom today at http://www.writewaysolutions.com.

Made in the USA
Charleston, SC
01 June 2012